Ancient Battlefields

Ancient Battlefields

Conflict Sites in Northwestern England
from the Roman Period to 937A.D.

Charles Hardwick

LEONAUR

Ancient Battlefields
Conflict Sites in Northwestern England from the Roman Period to 937 A.D.
by Charles Hardwick

First published under the title
Ancient Battlefields

Leonaur is an imprint of Oakpast Ltd

ISBN: 978-1-78282-066-6 (hardcover)
ISBN: 978-1-78282-067-3 (softcover)

http://www.leonaur.com

Publisher's Notes

Contents

To
George Milner, Esq., President,
and to the Council and Members of the
Manchester Literary Club,
This Work is Respectfully Inscribed by
One of Its Founders.
Charles Hardwick.

Preface

To the transactions of the Manchester Literary Club (1875-8) I contributed four papers on "Some Ancient Battlefields in Lancashire." These essays form the *nuclei* of the four chapters of the present volume. Their original scope, however, has been much extended, and the evidences there adduced largely augmented. I have likewise endeavoured to still further fortify and illustrate my several positions, by citations from well-known, and many recent, labourers in similar or cognate fields of enquiry.

I am aware that the precise locality of any given battlefield is of relatively little interest to the general historian, the causes of the conflict and its political results demanding the largest share of his attention. Consequently, doubtful topographical features are often either completely ignored, or but slightly referred to. Such a course, however, is not permissible to the local student. Scarcely anything can be too trifling, in a certain sense, to be unworthy of some investigation on his part. This is especially the case with respect to legendary stories, and traditional beliefs. Their interest is intensified, it is true, to the local reader or student, but the lessons they teach, on patient enquiry, will often be found in harmony with larger or more general truths, and of which truths they often form apt illustrations.

"Verax," exclaimed truly in one of his recent letters in the *Manchester Weekly Times:*

> Alas! it is hard to disengage ourselves from inherited illusions. They become a part of our being, and falsify the standard of comparison.

Modern science may be able to demonstrate that many of the conceptions respecting physical phenomena dealt with in these legendary stories are utterly at variance with now well-known facts. This may be perfectly true, but human nature is influenced in its action, quite as much by its faiths, beliefs, and superstitions, as by the more exact knowledge it may have acquired. Subjective truths are as true, as mere facts or actualities, as objective ones.

Thomas Carlyle forcibly expresses this when he asks—

Was Luther's picture of the devil *less a reality*, whether it were formed within the bodily eye, or without it?

Mr. J. R. Green, in his *Making of England*, says—

Legend, if it distorts facts, preserves accurately enough the *impressions* of a vanished time."

And these impressions being emotionally true, whether scientifically correct or not, have ever been, and will continue to be, powerful factors in the formation of character, and in the progressive development of humanity,—morally, socially, and politically. Our predecessors felt their influence and acted accordingly, and many of the presumedly exploded old superstitions survive amongst the mass of mankind to a much greater degree than we often acknowledge or even suspect; although many of their more repulsive forms may have undergone superficial transformation amongst the more educated classes.

Referring to superstitious legendary reverence as a marked feature in the religious characteristics of the seventeenth century, the author of *John Inglesant, a Romance*, places in the mouth of the rector of the English College, at Rome, in the seventeenth century, the following words:—"These things are true to each of us according as we see them; they are, in fact, but shadows and likenesses of the absolute truth that reveals itself to man in different ways, but always imperfectly, as in a glass."

The *Anglo-Saxon Chronicle* records that, in the year 685, "it rained blood in Britain, and milk and butter were turned into blood." Of course, educated persons do not believe this *now*; but our conventionally educated predecessors did, and their conduct was sensibly influenced by such belief. The Chinese think themselves much superior personages, in very many respects, to the "barbarian" European, yet the following paragraph "went the round of the papers" during May, in the present year:—

The Kaiping coal mines have been closed in deference to the opinion expressed by the Censor, that the continued working of them would release the earth dragon, disturb the manes of

10

the empress, and bring trouble upon the imperial family.

From the very nature of many of the subjects investigated, and the character of the only available evidence, some of the inferences drawn in the following pages can only be regarded as probabilities, and others as merely possibilities, and they are put forth with no higher pretensions. In such matters dogmatical insistence is out of place, and I have studiously endeavoured to avoid it.

C. H.

72, Talbot Street, Moss Side, Manchester.
August, 1882.

CHAPTER 1

Early Historical and Legendary Battles

It has often been remarked, and with some truth, that our standard historical works, until very recent times at least, contained little more than the details of battles, the squabbles and intrigues of diplomatists and politicians, and the pedigrees of potentates, imperial or otherwise. Nowadays we seek to know more of the domestic habits and conditions of the mass of the population, and the degree and kind of intellectual and moral culture which obtained amongst a people at any given period of their history. But man's advance from the savage to his present relatively civilized condition has been one of fierce and sanguinary strife, and the piratical and freebooting instincts which he inherited, along with some of his nobler attributes and aspirations, from his remote ancestors, are by no means extinguished at the present time, although, in their practical exhibition, they may generally assume a somewhat more decorous exterior.

Still, courage and physical endurance, however rude and uncouth in outward aspect, as well as heroism of a higher mental or moral order, ever possessed, and ever will possess, a strange and uncontrollable fascination; and the associations, social, political, or religious, attendant upon the more prominent of the bloody struggles of the past, excite, in a most powerful degree, the emotional as well as the imaginative elements of our being. This is notoriously the case when any special interest is superinduced, national or provincial.

All men naturally feel more interested in the historical associations of their own race than they do in those of any other portion of mankind. The soil daily trodden by the foot of any reflecting being,—the locality with whose present struggles, progress or decay, he is practically acquainted,—whose traditions and folk-lore were first fixed in his memory and his heart, long before more exact knowledge or cultivated judgment enabled him to test their accuracy or correctly weigh their value,—must possess historic reminiscences not only capable of commanding his attention, by exciting in the imaginative faculty agreeable and healthy sensations, but of teaching him valuable lessons in profound practical wisdom.[1]

It might be said, without much exaggeration, that if the soil could be endowed with vocal utterance, we might learn that the surface area of the earth which has *not* sustained the shock of battle at some period of the world's history is not very much greater than that which has felt the tread of armed men in deadly conflict. In the early historic and pre-historic times, when clan or sept fought, as a matter of course, against clan or sept, for the privilege of existence or the means to secure it; or when baron or other chieftain "levied private war" against his neighbour, from ambition, passion or greed, numberless fierce and bloody struggles must have taken place of which no record has been preserved.

The *names* of many important ancient battlefields have been handed down to the present time, the sites of which are either utterly unknown or involved in great obscurity. Some genuine historical events have been so inextricably interwoven with the mythical and traditionary legends of our forefathers, that it is now impossible to detect with exactness the residuum of historical truth therein contained. The battlefields and all authentic record of the battles themselves amongst the inhabitants of Britain prior to the Roman conquest are, of course, utterly lost in the gloom of the past. Nay, we know, with certainty, very few even of the sites of the struggles of the Britons with the victorious Roman legions.

The locality we now denominate Lancashire was, at that time, inhabited by the Volantii and the Sistuntii, Setantii, or Segantii, and was included in the "country of the Brigantes," a numerous and warlike tribe which frequently "measured blades" with the imperial troops. There exists, however, no record to inform us where any specific conflict took place, notwithstanding the numerous archaeological remains which attest the after-presence of the conquerors. Yet we know on

---

1. *His. Preston*, viii.

the best authority that the Brigantes espoused the cause of the Iceni, who inhabited the Norfolk of the present day, and were defeated by Ostorius Scapula, in the reign of Claudius.

Soon after the death of Galba, an insurrection broke out amongst them, headed by a chief named Venutius, who had married the Brigantine queen, Cartismandua, a woman infamous in British history as the betrayer of the brave but unfortunate Caractacus. This royal lady likewise played false with her husband, but Fortune refused to smile on her second perfidy. She escaped with difficulty to the territory occupied by her Roman allies, and Venutius remained master of the "country of the Brigantes," and for a considerable time successfully resisted the progress of the imperial arms. Petilius Cerealis, however, in the reign of Vespatian, after a sanguinary conflict, added the greater portion of the Brigantine territory to the Roman province. The final conquest was effected about the year 79, by Julius Agricola, in the reign of Domitian. Remains of stations established by him are numerous in Lancashire.

On Extwistle Moor, about five miles to the east of Burnley, and about the same distance south of Caster-cliff, a Roman station, near Colne, are the remains of two Roman camps and three tumuli. The sites are marked in the ordnance map. A few years ago, in company with my friend, the late T. T. Wilkinson, I visited this locality and inspected the remains. In the transactions of the Historic Society of Lancashire, for 1865-6, I described and figured an ancient British urn, taken from one of these *tumuli*. It was in the possession of the late Mr. R. Townley Parker, of Cuerden, the owner of the estate. In the same paper I have described and figured British remains, including about ten cremated interments and a bronze spear-head, found in a mound on the Whitehall estate, contiguous to Low Hill House, near Over Darwen, the property of Mr. Ellis Shorrock. Similar tumuli have been opened in several other places in the county, to which further reference will be made. From these remains it is not improbable some of the struggles of the Brigantes with the imperial legions took place in these localities, or they may have been ordinary burial places of distinguished chieftains and their relatives.

After the departure of the Roman legions and their attendant auxiliaries, history becomes inextricably allied to, and interwoven with, legend and romance. The marvellous narratives of the elder "historians," such as Gildas, Nennius, and Geoffrey of Monmouth, may have some substratum of fact underlying an immense mass of tradition,

15

superstition, and artistic fiction. In the endeavour to unravel this complicated web, much ingenuity and valuable time have been expended, with but relatively barren results, at least so far as the so-called "strictly historical element" is concerned. Mr. E. B. Tylor, in his *Researches into the Early History of Mankind and the Development of Civilization*, referring to the value of "Historical Traditions and Myths of Observation" to the ethnologist, says—

"His great difficulty in dealing with them is to separate the fact and the fiction, which are both so valuable in their different ways; and this difficulty is aggravated by the circumstance that these two elements are often mixed up in a most complex manner, myths presenting themselves in the dress of historical narrative, and historical facts growing into the wildest myths."

The reputed deeds of Arthur and his "Knights of the Round Table" have not only given birth to our most famous mediaeval romances, but they have furnished the laureate with themes for several of his more delightful poetic effusions. Professor Henry Morley, in his *English Writers*, regards Geoffrey's work as "a natural issue of its time, and the source of one of the purest streams of English poetry." Indeed, it appears to be the opinion of many scholars, including Mr. J. D. Harding, Rev. T. Price, and Sig. Panizzi, late chief librarian of the British Museum, that the entire European cycle of romance "originated in Welsh invention or tradition." The last named, in his *Essay on the Narrative Poetry of the Italians*, prefixed to his edition of Boiardo and Ariosto, distinctly states that "all the chivalrous fictions since spread through Europe appear to have had their birth in Wales."

Mr. Fiske, of Harvard University, in his *Myths and Myth-makers*, referring to the Greek tradition concerning the "Return of the Herakleids," says:

It is undoubtedly as unworthy of credit as the legend of Hengist and Horsa; yet, like the latter, it doubtless embodies a historical occurrence.

Such may likewise be the case with some of the battles known from tradition to the early story-tellers, poets, or romance writers, who crystallized, as it were, all their floating warlike legends around the names of Arthur and his knights. Our mediaeval ancestors, with very few isolated exceptions, innocently accepted Geoffrey's wild assertions as sober historical facts, notwithstanding the gross ignorance and falsehood patent in many passages, and the childish superstition and credulity which characterise others. Indeed, only about a century ago, the Rev. Jno. Whitaker, the historian of Manchester, placed so much faith in the statements of Nennius and Geoffrey, that he regarded their Arthur as a really historical personage, and he fixed the sites of several of his presumed exploits in the county of Lancaster.

There may undoubtedly have existed, nay, there probably did exist, a British chieftain who fought against Teutonic invaders during some portion of the two or three centuries occupied in the Anglo-Saxon conquest, whose name was Arthur, but his deeds, whatever may have been their extent or character, have been so exaggerated and interwoven with far more ancient mythical stories, and confounded with those of other warriors, that his individuality or personality, in a truly *historical* sense, is apparently lost.

Indeed, Mr. Haigh expressly says—

There was another Arthur, a son of Mouric, king of Glamorgan, mentioned in the register of Llandaff.

In his *History of the Conquest of Britain by the Saxons*, by altering the time of the "coming of the Angles" to *A.D.* 428, "in accordance with a date supplied by the earliest authority," and of the accession of Arthur to *A.D.* 467. He contends that:—

. . . . . in accordance with a date given by other authorities, all anachronisms—involved in the system which is based upon the dates in the *Saxon Chronicle* and the *Annals of Cambria,*—have disappeared one after another; every successive event has fallen into its proper place; the *Saxon Chronicle* and the *Brut* have been proved accordant; and the result is a perfectly connected and consistent history, such as has never yet been expected, vindicating the truth of our early historians, and showing that authentic materials formed the substance of their Chronicles.

In another place he contends that, by adapting his chronology, "a foundation of historic truth" is discovered "in stories which have hitherto been looked upon as mere romances."[2]

Notwithstanding this conviction, Mr. Haigh does not assume that all the legendary lore which has attached itself to the name of Arthur is of this character. Referring to the traditionary tomb of the hero, he thus fearlessly exposes the medieval imposture which sought to

---

2. Mr. Haigh's ingenious hypothesis, however, is not accepted by historical students generally.

demonstrate the truth of the legend:—

An ancient sepulchre, intended by those who were interested in the search to prove itself the sepulchre of Arthur, was opened in *A.D.* 1189 (the last year of Henry II. and most probably the first of Abbot Henry de Soilly, under whom the search was made), in the cemetery at Glastonbury. There was on the one hand a superstition that he was not dead, and on the other a tradition that he was buried at Glastonbury; and it was the policy of Henry II. to establish the truth of the latter; and a search was ordered to be made in a spot which was sure to be crowned with success by the discovery of an interment.

It was recognized as a sepulchre; indeed, distinctly marked as such by the pyramids (tapering pillar-stones), one at either end,—objects of curious interest on account of their venerable antiquity; and William of Malmsbury, thirty years before, (at a time when no suspicion that Arthur was buried there existed at Glastonbury), had recorded his belief that the bodies of those whose names were written on the monuments were contained in stone coffins within. To prove that this was the sepulchre of Arthur, nothing more was necessary than to forge an inscription, which might impose upon the credulity of the twelfth century, but which the archaeological science of the nineteenth must condemn.

The cross of lead, which served to identify the remains of Arthur and his queen is lost, but a representation of it has been preserved, sufficiently to show that its form and character were precisely such as were usual in the twelfth century, such as those discovered in the coffins of Prior Aylmer (who died *A.D.* 1137), and of Archbishop Theobald (who died *A.D.* 1161), and in the cemetery of Bouteilles, near Dieppe, present. The pyramids appear to have resembled the Bewcastle and Ruthwell monuments; their age is determined by the names of King Centwine and Bishop Hedde,[3] inscribed on the smaller one; to have been

---

3. "It was twenty-six feet high, and had inscribed on it these names, and two others, Bregored and Beorward. Centwine became King of the West Saxons, and Hedde, Bishop of Winchester, in A.D. 676; the former became a monk in *A.D.* 683, the latter died in *A.D.* 705. Bregored was an Abbot of Glastonbury (but not in the times of the Britons, as William of Malmsbury concluded from his name, for it is clearly Saxon), and Beorward may be the Abbot Beornwald who attested a charter of Ine in *A.D.* 704. The larger pyramid, twenty-eight feet high, (continued next page),

the close of the seventh, or the beginning of the eighth century; and as the skeleton of a man and a woman were found in coffins hollowed out of the trunks of oak trees, it is probable that they were those of Wulfred and Eanfled, whose names occur in the inscription on the larger one.

Welsh traditions and writers ignore the Glastonbury legend, and regard, in some way or other, Arthur as a being exempt from ordinary mortality. The Rev. R. W. Morgan, in his *Cambrian History*, says,—

His farewell words to his knights—'I go hence in God's time, and in God's time I shall return,' created an invincible belief that God had removed him, like Enoch and Elijah, to Paradise without passing through the gate of death; and that he would at a certain period return, reascend the British throne, and subdue the whole world to Christ. The effects of this persuasion were as extraordinary as the persuasion itself, sustaining his countrymen under all reverses, and ultimately enabling them to realise its spirit by placing their own line of the Tudors on the throne. As late as *A.D.* 1492, it pervaded both England and Wales. 'Of the death of Arthur, men yet have doubt,' writes Wynkyn de Worde, in his chronicle, 'and shall have for evermore, for as men say none wot whether he be alive or dead.' The *aphanismus* or disappearance of Arthur is a cardinal event in British history. The pretended discovery of his body and that of his queen Ginevra, at Glastonbury, was justly ridiculed by the Kymri as a Norman invention. Arthur has left his name to above six hundred localities in Britain.

Mr. Haigh, whilst maintaining the substantial historical veracity of Arthur's invasion of France, nevertheless adds:

When we consider how miserably the history of the Britons has been corrupted, in the several editions through which it has passed, we cannot expect otherwise than that the Brut should have suffered through the blunders of scribes, and the occa-

---

which stood at the head of the grave, is said to have been in a very ruinous condition, and the only intelligible words in the inscription upon it (as given by William of Malmsbury), are the names of Wulfred and Eanfled. The discovery of these trunk coffins at Glastonbury has not been noticed by Mr. Wright, in his account of the similar discoveries at Gristhorpe, Beverley, Driffield, and Selby (*Gent. Mag.* 1857. vol. ii. p. 114), nor by Mr. Wylie in his paper on the Oberflacht graves (*Archæologia*, vol. xxxvi., p. 129), but deserves to be mentioned in connection with them."

sional introduction of marginal notes, and even of extraneous matter into the text, in the course of six centuries. Such an interpolation, I believe, is the story of an adventure with a giant, with which Arthur is said to have occupied his leisure, whilst waiting for his allies at Barbefleur; and I think the reference to another giant-story (not in the *Brut*), with which it concludes, marks it as such. But I am convinced that the story of the Gallic campaign is a part of the original *Brut*, and is substantially true.

Dr. James Fergusson, in his learned and elaborate work on the *Rude Stone Monuments of all Countries*, although stoutly contending for the historical verity of the victories ascribed to Arthur by Nennius, somewhat brusquely rejects the Lancashire sites, because, on his visit to the localities indicated by Whitaker and others, he found no megalithic remains to support his ingenious hypothesis respecting battlefield memorials. He says:

> I am much more inclined to believe that Linnuis is only a barbarous Latinization of Linn, which in Gaelic and Irish means sea or lake. In Welsh it is Lyn, and in Anglo-Saxon Lin, and if this is so, '*In regione Linnuis*' may mean in the Lake Country.

However, he confesses he can find no River Duglas in that district, and in another sentence he regards the nearness of the sea to Wigan as an objectionable element on military grounds. I hold a contrary view. A defeated commander near Wigan had the great Roman road for retreat either to the north or south, besides the vicinal ways to Manchester and Ribchester. The objection, moreover, is valueless, from the simple fact that battles *have* been fought in the localities, as is attested both by historic records and discovered remains.

Henry of Huntingdon, who wrote in the earlier portion of the twelfth century, regarded Arthur as a genuine historical character, and attributed the then ignorance of precise localities of the twelve battles described by Nennius to "the Providence of God having so ordered it that popular applause and flattery, and transitory glory, might be of no account."

William of Malmsbury, in the twelfth century, although evidently aware of the legendary character of the mass of the Arthurian stories, seems, however, to have had some confidence that a substratum of historic truth underlying or permeating the mass, might, with skill and diligence, eventually be extracted. Probably a few years before Geoffrey's work appeared, he writes—

That Arthur, about whom the idle tales of the Bretons (*nugæ Britonum*) craze to this day, one worthy not to have misleading fables dreamed about him, but to be celebrated in true history, since he sustained for a long time his tottering country, and sharpened for war the broken spirit of his people.

It is a remarkable circumstance that Shakespeare, who has availed himself so profusely of the old historic and legendary records, as well as of the popular superstitions, with two trivial exceptions, which merely prove his acquaintance with the traditional hero, never refers to Arthur. The exceptions are so slight and even casual that they seem rather to confirm the probability that the great poet, in the main, endorsed the opinion of William of Newbury as to Geoffrey's presumed *historical* verities. This critical monk, in the latter portion of the twelfth century, indignantly exclaims:

Moreover, in his book, that he calls the *History of the Britons*, how saucily and how shamelessly he lies almost throughout, no one, unless ignorant of the old histories, when he falls upon that book can doubt. Therefore in all things we trust Bede, whose wisdom and sincerity are beyond doubt, so that fabler with his fables shall be straightway spat out by us all.

The fact that the story of *Lear* is given pretty fully in Geoffrey's work in no way affects this conclusion, as Shakespeare, in the construction of his plot, has followed an older drama and a ballad rather than the *soi-disant* Welsh historian. One allusion by Shakespeare to Arthur is in the second part of *Henry IV.* (Act 3, Scene 2), where Justice Shallow says:

I remember at Mile-end Green (when I lay at Clement's Inn, I was then Sir Dagonet in Arthur's Show)," &c. The other is in Act 2, Scene 4, of the second part of King Henry IV., when Falstaff enters the tavern in Eastcheap singing a scrap of an old ballad, as follows: "'*When Arthur first in court*'—Empty the jordan—'*And was a worthy king*'—[Exit Drawer.]—How now, Mistress Doll?

Sir Edward Strachey, in his introduction to the Globe edition of Sir Thomas Malory's *Morte D'Arthur*, confesses that it is impossible to harmonise the geography of the work. This, however, is a very ordinary condition in most legendary stories, literary or otherwise. Speaking of the renowned Caerleon on Usk, he says—

It seems through this, as in other romances, to be inter-change-able in the author's mind with Carlisle, or (as written in its Anglo-Norman form) Cardoile, which latter, in the History of Merlin, is said to be in Wales, whilst elsewhere Wales and Cumberland are confounded in like manner. So of Camelot, where Arthur chiefly held his court, Caxton in his preface speaks as though it were in Wales, probably meaning Caerleon, where the Roman amphitheatre is still called Arthur's Round Table.

Other geographical elements in the work are even more unsatisfactory. There is, indeed, a Carlion and a Cærwent referred to in the Breton lai d'Ywenec, and the latter is said to be "on the Doglas," and was the capital city of Avoez, "lord of the surrounding country." Even, if the scene of the Breton romance be presumed to be in the present Monmouthshire, where we yet find the names Caerleon and Caerwint, still we have a claimant in the Scottish Douglas, as well as in the Lancashire river of that name.

Mr. J. R. Green, in his recently published work, *The Making of England*, says

Mr. Skene, who has done much to elucidate these early struggles, has identified the sites of" (Arthurian) "battles with spots in the north (see his *Celtic Scotland*, i. 153-154, and more at large his *Four Ancient Books of Wales*, i. 55-58); but as Dr. Guest has equally identified them with districts in the south, the matter must still be looked upon as somewhat doubtful.

The doubt is increased by the fact that Hollingworth, Mr. Haigh, the Rev. John Whitaker, and others, as well as local tradition, with equal confidence have identified some of the struggles with the Lancashire battlefields now under consideration.

Dr. Sir G. Webbe Dasent, in his review of Dr. Latham's *Johnson's Dictionary*, referring to the struggles of the ancient Britons with their Anglo-Saxon invaders, has the following very pertinent observations:—

After the Roman legions left the Britons to themselves, there is darkness over the face of the land from the fifth to the eighth century. Those are really our dark ages. From 420, when it is supposed that Honorius withdrew his troops, to 730, when Bede wrote his history, we see nothing of British history. Afar off we hear the shock of arms, but all is dim, as it were, when two mighty hosts do battle in the dead of night. When the dawn comes and the black veil is lifted, we find that Britain has passed away. The land is now England; the Britons themselves, though still strong in many parts of the country, have been generally worsted by their foes; they have lost that great battle which has lasted through three centuries. Their Arthur has come and gone, never again to turn the heady fight.

Henceforth Britain has no hero, and merely consoles herself with the hope that he will one day rise and restore the fortunes of his race. But, though there were many battles in that dreary time, and many Arthurs, it was rather in the everyday battle of life, in that long unceasing struggle which race wages with race, not sword in hand alone, but by brain and will and feeling, that the Saxons won the mastery of the land. Little by little, more by stubbornness and energy than by bloodshed, they spread themselves over the country, working towards a common unity, from every shore. . . . Certain it is that for a long time after the time of Bede, and therefore undoubtedly before his day, the Celtic and Saxon kings in various parts of the island lived together on terms of perfect equality, and gave and took their respective sons and daughters to one another in marriage.

The Arthur of romance is, in fact, the artistic creation of writers of a later age, or, indeed, of later ages, than the conquest of Britain by the Anglo-Saxons, and not of contemporary historians, bardic or otherwise. The British chieftain who fought against Ida and his Angles in the north of England, and whose territory, including that of subordinate chieftains or allies, is believed at one time to have extended from the Clyde to the Ribble, or even the Dee, with an uncertain boundary on the east, is named Urien of Rheged, the district north of the Solway estuary, including the modern Annandale. He is the great hero of the Welsh bard Taliesin. Amongst his other qualities the poet enumerates the following:

> Protector of the land, usual with thee is headlong activity and the drinking of ale, and ale for drinking, and fair dwelling and beautiful raiment.

Llywarch Hen, or the Old, another Keltic poet, who lived between *A.D.* 550-640, incidentally mentions Arthur as a chief of the Kymri of the South, thus, as Professor Henry Morley puts it: "What Urien was in the north Arthur was in the south." This may well account for the geographical discrepancies referred to by Sir Edward Strachey. Llywarch Hen was present at the bloody battle in which his lord, Geraint (one of the knights introduced into the succeeding romances), and a whole host of British warriors perished. The said bard likewise brought away the head of Urien in his mantle, after his decapitation by the sword of an assassin. In the early English metrical romance, *Merlin*, a Urien, King of Scherham, father of the celebrated Ywain, is mentioned as the husband of Igerna's third daughter by her first husband, Hoel.

Urien, of Rheged, is mentioned, however, in the same romance as one of the competitors with Arthur for the crown of Britain. In Sir Thomas Malory's *Morte D'Arthur*, a "King Uriens of Gore" is introduced. "Gore" is evidently the Peninsula of Gower, in Glamorganshire, South Wales. These, however, are merely some of the geographical discrepancies referred to by Sir Edward Strachey; but such discrepancies, owing to the intermixture of several legends, under the circumstances, are inevitable, and are in themselves evidences of the lack of unity in the original sources from which the romance writers drew their materials.

Nennius's *History of Britain* was written, according to some authorities, at the end of the eighth century. Others ascribe it, in the condition at least in which we have it at present, with more probability, to the end of the tenth. Geoffrey of Monmouth's work was published in the twelfth. He professes, indeed, to have, to some extent, translated from an ancient manuscript, brought by "Walter, Archdeacon of Oxford," out of Brittany. This, however, notwithstanding Geoffrey's deliberate assertion, is doubted and even flatly denied by many competent judges. Be this as it may, no such document is otherwise known or indeed referred to by any reliable authority. If it ever existed, from its inherent defects, it can to us possess little strictly historical value, whatever amount of truthful legendary or traditional matter it may have furnished to the author of the so-called *Historia Britonum*. Referring to the too common habit of regarding mere tradition as reliable history, Mr. Fiske, in his review of Mr. Gladstone's *Juventus Mundi*, justly exclaims:

One begins to wonder how many more times it will be necessary to prove that dates and events are of no *historical* value unless attested by nearly contemporary evidence.

Now, one of the most significant facts in connection with this investigation is that neither Bede nor Gildas makes any mention of Arthur. Mr. Stevenson, in the preface to his edition of Gildas's work, in the original Latin, says:

> We are unable to speak with certainty as to his parentage, his country, or even his name, or of the works of which he was the author.

The title of the old English translation, however, is as follows:

> The Epistle of Gildas, the most ancient British author: who flourished in the yeere of our Lord, 546. And who, by his great erudition, sanctitie, and wisdome, acquired the name of *Sapiens*.

Bede was born in the year 673, and died in 735. The Rev. R. W. Morgan (*Cambrian History*) says:

> The genuine works of Aneurin—his *British History*, and *Life of Arthur*,—are lost; the work of Gildas, which at one time passed for the former is a forgery by Aldhelm, the Roman Catholic monk of Malmesbury.

If ever Arthur lived in the flesh it must have been in the fifth or sixth centuries, and yet, as I have previously observed, these writers make no reference whatever to the renowned king and warrior. So that, even if we grant the earlier assumed date to the work of Nennius, about three centuries must have elapsed between the performance of his deeds and their earliest known record! In Geoffrey of Monmouth's case the interval is no less than seven hundred years! Mr. John R. Green (*The Making of England*) says:

> The genuineness of Gildas, which has been doubted, may now be looked upon as established (see Stubbs and Haddan, *Councils of Britain*, i. p. 44). Skene (*Celtic Scotland*, i. 116, note) gives a critical account of the various biographies of Gildas. He seems to have been born in 516, probably in the north Welsh valley of the Clwyd; to have left Britain for Armorica when thirty years old, or in 546; to have written his history there about 556 or 560; to have crossed to Ireland between 566-569; and to have died there in 570. . . . Little, however, is to be gleaned from the confused rhetoric of Gildas; and it is only here and there that we can use the earlier facts which seem to be embedded among the later legends of Nennius.

Mr. Haigh, however, contends that an "earlier S. Gildas" was a relative of Arthur, and was born about *A.D.*425. He says—

He had written, so a British tradition preserved by Giraldus Cambrensis (twelfth century) informs us, noble books about the acts of Arthur and his race, but threw them into the sea when he heard of his brother's death; (at the hands of Arthur) and this tradition he says satisfactorily explains—what has been made the ground of an argument against the genuineness of the works ascribed to him—his studied silence with regard to Arthur.

Mr. Haigh likewise conjectures that *Nennius's History of the Britons* was written by St. Albinus, from contemporary records which had been carried to Armorica (Brittany), and subsequently lost. However, neither traditions first recorded seven centuries after the events transpired, nor "lives" of early British saints, are considered very trustworthy historical authorities. It requires very little knowledge of the state of literature, either in England or elsewhere, during these long periods of time, to remove any lingering doubt as to the purely legendary character of much of the contents of these books, even if we grant, as in the case of the Venerable Bede, that the authors themselves honestly related that which they honestly, however foolishly, believed to be true. Singularly enough, according to Spurrell's dictionary, the modern Welsh word *aruthr* signifies "marvellous, wonderful, prodigious, strange, dire," which is not without significance.

Nennius says:—

A.D. 452. Then it was that the magnanimous Arthur, with all the kings and military force of Britain, fought against the Saxons. And though there were *many more noble than himself*, yet he was twelve times chosen their commander, and was as often conqueror.

He then informs us that the second, third, fourth, and fifth of these battles were fought on the banks of a "river by the Britons called Duglas, in the region Linuis." Some copies give "Dubglas," which has been identified with the little stream Dunglas, which formed the southern boundary of Lothian. The Rev. John Whitaker, however, contends that the Douglas, in Lancashire, is the stream referred to. He advances, amongst much conjectural matter, the following archaeological and traditional details, in support of his position:—

The name of the river concurs with the tradition, and three battles prove the notice true.[4] On the traditionary scene of this engagement remained till the year 1770 a considerable British barrow, popularly denominated Hasty Knoll. It was originally a vast collection of small stones taken from the bed of the Douglas, and great quantities had been successively carried away by the neighbouring inhabitants. Many fragments of iron had been also occasionally discovered in it, together with the remains of those military weapons which the Britons interred with their heroes at death.

On finally levelling the barrow, there was found a cavity in the hungry gravel, immediately under the stones, about seven feet in length, the evident grave of the British officer, and all filled with the loose and blackish earth of his perished remains. At another place, near Wigan, was discovered about the year 1741 a large collection of horse and human bones, and an amazing quantity of horse-shoes, scattered over a large extent of ground—an evidence of some important battle upon the spot. The very appellation of Wigan is a standing memorial of more than one battle at that place.[5]

According to tradition, the first battle fought near Blackrode was uncommonly bloody, and the Douglas was crimsoned with blood to Wigan. Tradition and remains concur to evince the fact that a second battle was fought near Wigan Lane, many years before the *rencontre* in the civil wars. . . . The defeated Saxons appear to have crossed the hill of Wigan, where another engagement or engagements ensued; and in forming the canal there about the year 1735, the workmen discovered evident indications of a considerable battle on the ground.

All along the course of the channel, from the termination of the dock to the point at Poolbridge, from forty to fifty roods in length, and seven or eight yards in breadth, they found the

---

4. The Rev. E. Sibson says:—"A piece of high ground near the Scholes is called King Arthur's camp."—*Man. Lit. and Phil. Soc. Transactions, April*, 1845.

5. Giving a man "wigan," in the present vernacular of the county, is synonymous to giving him a good threshing.

Jacob Grimm, in his *Deutsche Mythologie*, says the Old High German *wig*, pugna, seems occasionally to denote the personal god of war.

The modern English word "vie," to contend, to fight, to strive for superiority, is derived from the Anglo-Saxon *wigian*, *wiggan*, which are cognate to the Gothic *veigan* (*Collins's Dic. Der.*) *Wig*, war, warfare, battle (*Bosworth, A.S. Dic.*)

ground everywhere containing the remains of men and horses. In making the excavations, a large old spur, carrying a stem four or five inches in length, and a rowel as large as a half-crown, was dug up; and five or six hundred weight of horse-shoes were collected. The point of land on the south side of the Douglas, which lies immediately fronting the scene of the last engagement, is now denominated the Parson's Meadow; and tradition very loudly reports a battle to have been fought in it.

The rev. historian of Manchester, referring to the statements in Nennius, thus sums up his argument:—

These four battles were fought upon the river Douglas, and in the region Linuis. In this district was the whole course of the current from its source to the conclusion, and the words, 'Super flumen quod vocatur Duglas, quod est in Linuis,' shows the stream to have been less known than the region. This was therefore considerable; one of the cantreds or great divisions of the Sistuntian kingdom, and comprised, perhaps, the western half of South Lancashire. From its appellation of Linuis or the Lake, it seems to have assumed the denomination from the Mere of Marton, (Martin) which was once the most considerable object in it.

The Rev. R. W. Morgan, in his *Cambrian History*, locates the Arthurian victories as follows:—

1st, at Gloster; 2nd, at Wigan (The Combats), 10 miles from the Mersey. The battle lasted through the night. In *A.D.*1780, on cutting through the tunnel, three cart loads of horse-shoes were found and removed; 3rd, at Blackrode; 4th, at Penrith, between the Loder and Elmot, on the spot still called King Arthur's Castle; 5th, on the Douglas, in Douglas Vale; 6th, at Lincoln; 7th, on the edge of the Forest of Celidon (Ettrick Forest) at Melrose; 8th, at Cær Gwynion; 9th, between Edinburgh and Leith; 10th, at Dumbarton; 11th, at Brixham, Torbay; 12th, at Mont Baden, above Bath.

Geoffrey of Monmouth refers but to one battle on the banks of the "Duglas." This he fixes at about the year 500. He tells us that:

The Saxons had invited over their countrymen from Germany, and, under the command of Colgrin, were attempting to exterminate the whole British race.... Hereupon, assembling the youth under his command, he marched to (towards) York, of which when Colgrin had intelligence, he met him with a very great army, composed of Saxons, Scots, and Picts, by the River Duglas, where a battle happened, with the loss of the greater part of both armies. Notwithstanding, the victory fell to Arthur, who pursued Colgrin to York, and there besieged him.

Mr. Daniel H. Haigh, one of the latest advocates of the genuine historical veracity which underlies much of the Arthurian traditions, places, as we have previously observed, Arthur's coronation *A.D.* 467, or about 32 years earlier than the usually received date. He says—

The River Douglas, which falls into the estuary of the Ribble, is certainly that which is indicated here; (the second, third, fourth, and fifth victories referred to by Nennius) and although it was one of Arthur's tactics to get round his adversaries, so as to be able to attack them when least expected (which will account for the scene of this conflict being considerably to the west of the direct line from London to York), it is extremely improbable that he would have gone so far north as the Douglas in Lothian, when his object was to attack Colgrin at York. The reading which the Paris MS. and Henry of Huntington give is, I believe, correct, and represents Ince, a name which is retained to this day by a township near to this river, a little more than a mile to the south-west of Wigan, and by another about fifteen miles to the west, and which may possibly have belonged to a considerable tract of country.[6] . . .

Neither the *Brut* nor Boece mention more than one battle at this time; but the latter says that Arthur 'pursued the Saxons, continually slaughtering them, until they took refuge in York,' and that 'having had so frequent victories he there besieged them;' and these expressions may well imply the four victories, gained in one prolonged contest on the Douglas, and another on the River Bassas, *i.e.*, Bashall brook, which falls into the Ribble near Clithero, in the direct line of Colgrin's flight to York.

If, therefore, the historical hypothesis be accepted, the Lancashire sites for these battles would seem as probable as any of the many others suggested.

---

6. The district referred to is variously written *Linuis, Cinuis,* and *Inniis.*

From the remains described by Whitaker, it appears certain that some great battles in early times have been fought on the banks of the Douglas, traditions concerning which may have served for the foundation of the after statements of Nennius and others. There are some recorded historical facts which countenance this view. The British warrior, king of the Western Britons, Cadwallon or Cadwalla,[7] with his ally, Penda, defeated and slew Edwin, King of Northumbria, uncle of St. Oswald, in the year 633, at Heathfield.[8] Where Heathfield is we have no perfectly satisfactory evidence.[9] The Brit-Welsh poet, Lywarch Hen, or the Old, a prince of the Cumbrian Britons, celebrated his praises in song. He says—

Fourteen great battles he fought,
For Britain the most beautiful,
And sixty skirmishes.

It is by no means improbable that some of Cadwalla's exploits, mythical as well as real, have become inextricably interwoven with the legendary ones of the heroes of the Arthurian romances. Singularly enough a paragraph in Geoffrey of Monmouth's work would seem to countenance this. In book 12, chapter 2, of his so-called *History of Britain*, he refers to negotiations being entered into and afterwards broken off, in the year 630, by Cadwalla and Edwin, while their armies lay on the opposite banks of *the River Douglas*, the scene of the presumed Arthurian victory over Colgrin in the year 500, according to the same authority. This circumstance is not without significance, as the legendary Arthur has evidently absorbed no inconsiderable portion of the reputations, in the North of England, of Urien of Rheged, and other veritable British warriors. Indeed, Lappenberg says—

The Welsh historians adopted the policy of *purloining from a successful enemy*, and skilfully transferring to his British contemporaries, if not to *imaginary personages*, the object and reward of his battles, the glory and lastingness of his individuality in history.

And, as illustrations of this practice, Mr. Daniel H. Haigh, in his *Conquest of Britain by the Saxons*, adds:

---

7. Nennius calls him "Catgublaun, king of Guenedot," Gwynedd, North Wales.
8. Anglo-Saxon Chron. and Bede.
9. Dr. Giles, Mr. Green, and others, say—"Hatfield, in the West Riding of Yorkshire, about seven miles to the north-east of Doncaster," and this seems the most probable site.

Thus, Cœdwealha, Ine, and Ivar are claimed by them as Cadwaladyr, Inyr, and Ivor.

Mr. Haigh, notwithstanding his faith in the substantial accuracy of much of the contents of the works of doubtful authority, says—

The peace which Ambrosius established was broken in the following year, *A.D.* 444. The Brut says nothing of this affair; it rarely records the defeats of the Britons.

And, similarly, the *Saxon Chronicle* is equally reticent in the opposite direction!

Indeed, this weakness is not exclusively an attribute of either British or Anglo-Saxon historians or romance writers. Mr. H. H. Howorth, in his able essay on *The Early History of Sweden*, in Vol. 9 of the *Transactions of the Royal Historical Society,* lucidly expounds the character of the contents of the professedly *Danish History by Saxo-Grammaticus.* He says—

He had no scaffolding upon which to build his narrative. He had to construct one for himself in the best way he could, and to piece together the various fragments before him into a continuous patchwork. His was not a critical age, and we are not therefore surprised to find that his handiwork was exceedingly rude. A piece of the history of the Lombards by Paul and Deacon, and another taken from the Edda, are thrust in after narratives evidently relating to the ninth century, when Ireland had been more or less conquered by the Norsemen. Icelanders are introduced into the story a long time before the discovery of Iceland.

Christianity is professed by Danish kings long before it had reached the borders of Denmark. The events belonging to one Harald (Harald Blatand) are transferred to another Harald who lived two or three centuries earlier, and the joints in the patchwork narrative are filled up by the introduction of plausible links. . . . . . The other important fact to remember is that our author was patriotic enough to lay under contribution, not only materials relating to Denmark, but to *transfer to Denmark the history of other countries.* To appropriate not only the traditions of the Anglo-Saxons, the Lombards, and the common Scandinavian heritage of the Edda, but also the particular histories of Sweden and Norway, and that a good deal of what passes for Danish history in his pages is not Danish at all, but Swedish, and relates to the rulers of Upsala, and not to those of Lethra; topographical boundaries being as lightly skipped over by the patriotic old chronicler, whose home materials were so scanty, as chronological ones.

It is, under such circumstances, vain to expect reliable historical evidence of the identity of locality or the names of the real warrior chiefs who commanded in many of the presumed Arthurian battles and adventures, some of them being evidently mythical or artistic creations. Whitaker's "large old spur, carrying a stem four or five inches in length, and a rowel as large as a half-crown," does not seem to indicate so early a date as the Anglo-Saxon conquests in Britain. Mr. Thomas Wright, in his *Celt, Roman and Saxon*, referring to spurs of the Roman, Saxon and Norman periods, says—

Amongst the extensive Roman remains found in the camp at Hod Hill were several spurs of iron, which resembled so closely the Norman prick-spurs, that they might easily be mistaken for them. I suspect that many of the prick-spurs which have been found on or near Roman sites, and hastily judged to be Norman, are, especially when made of bronze, Roman. As far, however, as comparison has yet been made, the *Roman and the Saxon spurs are shorter in the stimulus* than those of the Norman.

Spurs with long *stimuli* or large rowels do not appear to have been in use until sometime after the Norman Conquest. This, however, does not necessarily affect the antiquity of the whole of the remains referred to, which, of course, may have been deposited at different periods.

Hollingworth, in his *Mancuniensis*, written in the earlier portion of the seventeenth century, seems to have been aware of the existence of a tradition that referred to several bloody battles fought in Lancashire in some portion of the mysterious "olden time." He, however, assigns them to the period of the Roman conquest, to which I have previously referred. If the incidents in the Arthurian "romances" are no more historically tenable than those in the *Iliad* or the *Odyssey*, and as the Roman invasions of the Brigantine territory are undoubted, the elder Manchester historian's conjecture as to the time of the conflicts indicated by the tradition and the remains found near Wigan and Blackrod, may possibly be preferred to that of his successor, as the more probable of the two. Indeed, as has been previously observed, the romance writers and story-tellers have evidently absorbed and modified the historical traditions of many antecedent periods. Hollingworth says—

> In Vespatian's time Petilius Carealic" (Petilius Cerealis) "strooke a terror into the whole land by invading upon his first entry the Brigantes, the most populous of the whole province, many battailes, and bloody ones, were fought, and the greatest part of the Brigantes were either conquered or wasted.

Hollingworth, indeed, does afterwards refer to a battle near Wigan, in which he says Arthur was victorious. His words are—

> It is certaine that about *Anno Domini* 520, there was such a prince as King Arthur, and it is not incredible that hee or his knights might contest about this castle (Manchester) when he was in this country, and (as Nennius sayth) he put the Saxons to flight in a memorable battell neere Wigan, about twelve miles off.

Bishop Percy, in his introduction to the ancient ballad of *Chevy-Chase*, says—

> With regard to its subject, although it has no countenance from history, there is room to think that it had some foundation in fact....There had long been a rivalship between the two martial families of Percy and Douglas, which, heightened by the national quarrel, must have produced frequent challenges and struggles for superiority, petty invasions of their respective domains, and sharp contests for the point of honour, which would not always be recorded in history. Something of this kind we may suppose gave rise to the ancient ballad of the Hunting o' the Cheviat.
> The tragical circumstances recorded in the ballad are evidently borrowed from the Battle of Otterbourn, a very different event, *but which after times would easily confound with it....* Our poet has evidently jumbled the two events together.

During the seventh century many sanguinary encounters must have taken place in Lancashire, many of which are unrecorded, and the sites of others utterly forgotten. Professor Boyd-Dawkins, in a paper, entitled *On the Date of the Conquest of South Lancashire by the English*, read before the Manchester Literary and Philosophical Society, referring to the subjugation of what he aptly terms the "Brit-Welsh" of Strathclyde, (or the north-western part of the present England and the western portion of the lowlands of Scotland), by Ethelfrith, the powerful Northumbrian monarch, says that Chester was "the principal seat" of their power in that district. The whole of Lancashire, at this period, it would appear, was unconquered by the Angles or English. Under the date 607, the *Anglo-Saxon Chronicle* says—

> And this year Ethelfrith led his army to Chester, and there slew numberless Welshmen: and so was fulfilled the prophesy of Augustine, wherein he saith, 'If the Welsh will not be at peace with us, they shall perish at the hands of the Saxons.' There were also slain two hundred priests who came to pray for the army of the Welsh.

The death of these ecclesiastics, said to be monks of Bangor-Iscoed, was celebrated in song by a native poet. Florence of Worcester, referring to this battle, says:

> Ethelfrith first slew *twelve hundred* British priests, who had joined the army to offer prayers on their behalf, and then exterminated the remainder of this impious armament.

This is evidently an antagonistic priestly exaggeration, although other authorities state that the monastery at Bangor, at one time, contained 2,400 monks. This powerful body of Brit-Welsh Christians, according to Geoffrey of Monmouth, "disdained subjection to Augustine, and despised his preaching." Hence the strong clerical antipathy which characterised the conflict. Chester was utterly ruined, and is said to have remained desolate for about two centuries. Mr. Boyd Dawkins says—

> In all probability South Lancashire was occupied by the English at this time, and the nature of the occupation may be gathered from the treatment of the city of Chester. A fire, to use the metaphor of Gildas, went through the land, and the Brit-Welsh inhabitants were either put to the sword or compelled to become the bondsmen of the conquerors.

Mr. J. R. Green (*The Making of England*) traces Ethelfrith's march through Lancashire to his victory at Bangor-Iscoed. He says—

> Though the deep indent in the Yorkshire shire-line to the west proves how vigorously the Deirans had pushed up the river val-

leys into the moors, it shows that they had been arrested by the pass at the head of the Ribblesdale; while further to the south the Roman road that crossed the moors from York to Manchester was blocked by the unconquered fastnesses of Elmet, which reached away to the yet more difficult fastnesses of the Peak. But the line of defence was broken as the forces of Ethelfrith pushed over the moors along the Ribblesdale into our southern Lancashire. His march was upon Chester, the capital of Gwynedd, and probably the refuge place of Edwine.

The more northern portion of the county was not subdued till about half a century afterwards, when Cumberland and Westmoreland were absorbed into the Northumbrian kingdom by Ecgfrith (670-685). Mr. J. R. Green, in the work referred to, says—

The Welsh states across the western moors had owned, at least from Oswald's time, the Northumbrian supremacy, but little actual advance had been made by the English in this quarter since the victory of Chester, and northward of the Ribble the land between the moors and the sea still formed a part of the British kingdom of Cumbria. It was from this tract, from what we now know as northern Lancashire and the Lake District, Ecgfrith's armies chased the Britons in the early years of his reign.

Some severe struggles must have taken place during this period; and, therefore, it is by no means improbable that a portion, at least, of the remains on the banks of the Douglas, referred to by the Rev. John Whitaker as evidence of Arthur's historical existence, may pertain to the struggles of the Brit-Welsh and their Angle or English conquerors of the seventh century. This confusion of names and dates is a common feature in the folk-lore of all nations and periods, but in none is it more strongly developed than in the Arthurian romances. The author of the metrical *Morte D'Arthur*, after describing the victory of the hero over his rebellious nephew, Modred, at "Barren-down," near Canterbury, tells us that the barrows raised on the burial of the slain were still to be seen in his day. Barham Down is still covered with barrows, which recent examination has demonstrated to be the remains of a Saxon cemetery, and not a battlefield.

Bangor-Iscoed, the Bovium, and, at a later period, the Banchorium, of the Romans, is situated on the River Dee, some fourteen miles south of Chester. Sharon-Turner laments the destruction of its magnificent library at the sacking of the monastery, which he regarded as an "irreparable loss to the ancient British antiquities." Gildas, the *quasi*-historian, is said to have been one of its abbots. The Brit-Welsh commander during this struggle was Brocmail, the friend of Taliesin, who, in his poem on the disastrous battle, says—

> *I saw the oppression of the tumult; the wrath and tribulation;*
> *The blades gleaming on the bright helmets;*
> *The battle against the lord of fame, in the dales of Hafren;*
> *Against Brocvail[10] of Powys, who loved my muse.*

Sharon-Turner says the precise date of this battle is uncertain. The *Anglo-Saxon Chronicle* says it was fought in the year 607, and the Annals of Ulster in 612. Other authorities assign dates between the two.

The Rev, John Whitaker seems to have had not only a perfect faith in the historical existence of Arthur, but also of his famous knights of the "table round." Following tradition he locates at Castle-field, Manchester, the legendary fortress of "Sir Tarquin," a gigantic hero, to whose prowess several of Arthur's doughty knights had succumbed, before he himself fell beneath the stalwart arm of "Sir Lancelot du Lake." Whitaker regards Lancelot's patronymic, "du Lake," as referable to the Linius which gave the name to the district, according to the hypothesis previously advanced.

It is scarcely necessary to say that, notwithstanding all this ingenuity, Sir Tarquin, Sir Lancelot, and their knightly compeers, are as much creatures of the imagination as the heroes of any acknowledged work of fiction, such as the *Iliad* and the *Odyssey* of Homer, or the novels of Scott, Thackeray, Lord Lytton, and Dickens.

The *gradual growth* of what are generally regarded as the *spontaneous* products of the imagination, in the region of art, is well expressed in Mr. Tylor's admirable work on *Primitive Culture*. He says—

Amongst those opinions which are produced by a little knowledge, to be dispelled by a little more, is the belief in the almost boundless creative power in the human imagination. The superficial student, mazed in a crowd of seemingly wild and lawless fancies, which he thinks to have no reason in nature nor pattern in the material world, at first concludes them to be new births from the imagination of the poet, the tale-teller, and the seer. But little by little, in what seemed the most spontaneous fiction, a more comprehensive study of the source of

---

10. Variation, Brocmail.

poetry and romance begins to disclose a cause for each fancy, an education that has led up to each train of thought, a store of inherited materials from out of which each province of the poet's land has been shaped and built over and peopled.

Backward from our own times, the course of mental history may be traced through the changes wrought by modern schools of thought and fancy upon an intellectual inheritance handed down to them from earlier generations. And through remote periods, as we recede more nearly towards primitive conditions of our race, the threads which connect new thought with old do not always vanish from our sight. It is in large measure possible to follow them as clues leading back to that actual experience of nature and life which is the ultimate source of human fancy.

Perhaps no finer illustration, at least in English literature, of the truthfulness of this position can be cited than the Arthurian art-products with which I am dealing. In them we have embodied thoughts and fancies of the earlier myth-makers of our common Aryan race, legends and quasi-historical traditions of medieval times, the more artistic romances of a relatively recent and more highly-cultured period, and, lastly, the lyrics of Morris and others, and the splendid capital which worthily crowns this truly historic *literary* column, in the exquisitely felt and gracefully wrought *Idylls of the King*," by the laureate of the Victorian age, Alfred Tennyson. The last named says—

> *Lancelot spoke*
> *And answered him at full, as having been*
> *With Arthur in the fight which all day long*
> *Rang by the white mouth of the violent Glem:*
> *And in the four wild battles by the shore*
> *Of Douglas.*
>
> (*Idylls, p. 162.*)

Referring to the parentage of the Arthurian legends, in the essay prefixed to his *Specimens of Early English Metrical Romances*, Mr. George Ellis says—

> Although Geoffrey's *British Chronicle* is justly regarded as one of the corner-stones of romantic fiction, yet its principal, if not sole effect, was to stamp the names of Arthur, Merlin, Kay, and Gawain with the character of historical veracity; and thus to

37

authorise a collection of all the fables already current respecting these fanciful heroes and their companions. For not one word is to be found in that compilation concerning Sir Lancelot and his brothers; Sir Tristram; Sir Ywain; Joseph of Arimathea and the Sangrael; the round table with its perilous seat; and the various quests and adventures which fill so many folio volumes. These were subsequent additions, but additions *apparently derived from the same source*. The names, the manners of the heroes, and the scenes of their adventures, were still British; and, the taste for these strange traditions continuing to gain ground for at least two centuries, the whole literature of Europe was ultimately inundated by the nursery-tales of Wales and Armorica, as it had formerly been by the mythology of Greece and Egypt.

Of course there sometimes *is*, and there oftener *is not*, recognisable historical or biographical fact at the basis of so-called historical novels, poems, or plays, but the difficulty of separating the one from the other is generally insurmountable, and the labour bestowed thereon often profitless. This is especially the case where quasi-history has become inextricably interwoven with faded nature-myths and more modern artistic inventions. Mr. Fiske, in the work previously quoted, has the following very pertinent remarks on this subject:—

I do not suppose that the struggle between light and darkness was Homer's subject in the *Iliad* any more than it was Shakespeare's subject in *Hamlet*. Homer's subject was the wrath of the Greek hero, as Shakespeare's subject was the vengeance of the Danish prince. Nevertheless, the story of *Hamlet*, when traced back to its Norse original, is unmistakably the quarrel between summer and winter; and the moody prince is as much a solar hero as Odin himself. (See Simrock, *Die Quellen des Shakespeare*, I., 127-133.) Of course Shakespeare knew nothing of this, as Homer knew nothing of the origin of Achilleus. The two stories are therefore not to be taken *as sun-myths in their present form*.

They are the offspring of other stories which were sun-myths. They are stories which conform to the sun-myth type. . . . . The sun and the clouds, the light and the darkness, were once supposed to be actuated by wills analagous to the human will; they were personified and worshipped or propitiated by sacrifice; and their doings were described in language which applied so well to the deeds of human or quasi-human beings, that in course of time its primitive import faded from recollection. No competent scholar now doubts that the myths of the Veda and the Edda originated in this way, for philology itself shows that the names employed in them are the names of the great phenomena of nature.

And when once a few striking stories had thus arisen—when once it had been told how Indra smote the Panis, and how Sigurd rescued Brynhild, and how Odysseus blinded the Kyklops— then certain mythic or dramatic types hadd been called into existence; and to these types, preserved in the popular imagination, future stories would inevitably conform.... In this view I am upheld by a most sagacious and accurate scholar, Mr. E. A. Freeman, who finds in Carlovingian romance an excellent illustration of the problem before us.

The Carlovingian romance thus cited is, indeed, almost an exact counterpart of the Arthurian one, with the certainly very important exception that we can appeal to reliable history in the former case to prove our position, while the mythical gloom of legend and tradition obscures so much of the probable historical facts in connection with the latter that our path is beset with difficulties which cannot be solved otherwise than by analogical inference. History informs us of the acts and deeds of Karl der Gross, a German by birth, name, race, and language. This warrior, who conquered nearly the whole of Europe and founded one of the most important dynastic houses in medieval times, was born about the year 742, in the castle of Silzburg, in Bavaria, and died in 814 at Aachen, now called Aix-la-Chapelle.

On the other hand, as Mr. Fiske says:

The Charlemagne of romance is a mythical personage. He is supposed to be a Frenchman at a time when neither the French nation nor the French language can properly be said to have existed; and he is represented as a doughty crusader, although crusading was not thought of until long after the Karolingian era. He is a myth, and what is more he is a solar myth—an *avatar*, or at least a representative of Odin in his solar capacity. If in his case legend were not controlled by history, he would be for us as unreal as Agamemnon.... To the historic Karl corresponds in many particulars the mythical Charlemagne.

The legend has preserved the fact, which without the information supplied by history we might perhaps set down as a fiction, that there was a time when Germany, Gaul, Italy, and part of Spain formed a single empire. And as Mr. Freeman has well observed, the mythical crusades of Charlemagne are good evidence that there *were* crusades, although the real Karl had nothing whatever to do with one.

In the old ballad legend of Sir Guy, of Warwick, this chronological confusion is equally apparent. One of the earlier *stanzas* says—

Nine hundred twenty yeere and odde
After our Saviour Christ his birth,
When King Athelstone wore the crowne,
I lived heere upon the earth.

And yet this same legendary hero slays Saracens and other "heathen pagans" during the crusades some three centuries afterwards. The "*Scop*" or Geeman's song, and others, exhibit similar instances of this confusion of personages and dates.

Saxo Grammaticus, the Danish historian, has, like Geoffrey of Monmouth, mingled so much legendary and irrelevant matter with his genuine material, that it is often difficult and sometimes impossible to distinguish one from the other. Mr. H. H. Howorth, in the work previously quoted, referring to Harald Hildetand, "the most prominent figure in Scandinavian history at the close of the heroic period," says—

Although Saxo's notice of him is long, it will be found to contain scarcely anything about him. It is filled up with parenthetical stories about other people, referring doubtless to other times altogether, while the stories it contains about his exploits in Aquitania, and Britain, and Northumbria, show very clearly, as Müller has pointed out, that he has confused his doings with those of another, and much later, Harald, probably Harald Blaatand (*Op. Cit.* 366, note 3). It is only when we come to the close of his reign that we have a more detailed and valuable story. This is the account of the famous fight at Bravalla, of which we have two recensions, one in Saxo and the other in the Sogubrot, and which have preserved for us one of the most romantic epical stories in the history of the north.
The story was recorded in verse by the famous champion Starkadr, whom Saxo quotes as his authority, and whom he

seems closely to follow. Dahlman has, I think, argued very forcibly that the form and matter of this saga as told by Saxo is more ancient, and preserves more of the local colour of the original than that of the Sogubrot (*Forsch*, etc., 307–308).

And yet the story as it stands is very incongruous, and makes it impossible for us to believe that it was written by a contemporary at all. How can we understand Icelanders fighting in a battle a hundred years before Iceland was discovered, and what are we to make of such champions as Orm the Englishman, Brat the Hibernian, etc., among the followers of Harald? It would seem that on such points the story has been somewhat sophisticated, perhaps, as in the Roll of Battle Abbey, names have been added to flatter later heroes.

It is a recognised element in popular tradition or folk-lore, that the deeds of one historic or mythological hero are sure, when he is forgotten, to be attributed to some other man of mark, who, for the time being, fills the popular fancy. I am, therefore, inclined to think that the imaginary victories of Arthur on the continent of Europe in the sixth century, as recorded in Geoffrey's tenth book, owe their origin mainly to the real ones of Karl der Gross in the ninth. Geoffrey, or his Breton authority, had three centuries of tradition to fall back upon, time amply sufficient for medieval myth makers and romance writers to torture them to their own purposes. Instances of this re-crystallisation of several stories, mythical and otherwise, around the name of a single hero, by the vulgar, may be found in relatively modern history.

There is, in the region of traditional lore, in various parts of England, a mythical Cromwell, as well as the two well-known historical personages of that name. In whatever part of the country stands a ruined castle or abbey, or other ecclesiastical edifice, the nearest peasant, or even farmer, will assure an inquirer that it was battered into ruin by Oliver Cromwell! Here the Secretary Cromwell, of Henry the Eighth's reign, and the renowned Protector, of the following century, are evidently amalgamated. Indeed, the redoubted Oliver seems to have absorbed all the castle and abbey-destroying heroes of the national history, old Time himself included. There is a weather-worn statue on the triangular bridge at Croyland, erected in honour of King Ethelbald, the founder of the neighbouring abbey now in ruins, which is popularly supposed to be an effigy of Cromwell, and by some the bridge is likewise named after him. It is, however, more than probable that the neighbouring ruin is alone responsible for this nomenclature. A similar fate has befallen Alexander the Great in the East. Arminius Vámbéry, in his *Travels in Central Asia*, says—

> The history of the great Macedonian is invested by the Orientals with all the characteristics of a religious myth; and although some of their writers are anxious to distinguish Iskender Zul Karnein (the two-horned Alexander), the hero of their fable, from Iskenderi Roumi (the Greek Alexander), I have yet everywhere found that these two persons were regarded as one and the same.

There is likewise a mythical as well as an historical Taliesin (the Welsh poet), but they are generally confounded by the populace.

Mr. C. P. Kains-Jackson, in *Our Ancient Monuments and the Land around them*, referring to the huge rock, named "Arthur's Quoit," Gower, Llanridian, Glamorganshire, says—

> The reason why the name of Arthur should attach to the Titantic boulder represented in our engraving does not readily appear. The name has probably come by that process of accretion which has caused every witty cynicism to be attributed to Talleyrand, or, in another way, every achievement of the Third Crusade to Richard Cœur de Lion, and every contemporary woodland exploit to Robin Hood. No name from Druidical times attaching to the monument, the local tradition joined to the rock the name of the only man whose legendary repute and fame at all admitted of a super-human feat of strength being attributed to him.

Mr. Frederick Metcalfe, in his *Englishman and Scandinavian*, says—

> Then again our old institution, trial by jury, to our immortal King Alfred, the people's darling, it has been assigned, along with other tithings, hundreds, and a host of other inventions and institutions, which, we are persuaded, he would have been the first to repudiate. Indeed, he has become a sort of Odin to some antiquaries, on whom everything bearing the stamp of remote antiquity was gathered, the invention of names amongst the rest.

The same writer, referring to the "famous story of Theophilus," says—

The legend, as we have said, ran through Europe in various shapes, and was fitted to all people imaginable. It is referred to in one of Ælfric's homilies (*i.* 448), while in an Icelandic legend Anselm and Theophilus are thus blended. Now we know that Eormenric, who died 370, Attila, 453, Gundicar of Burgundy, 436, and the Ostrogothic King Theordoric or Dietrich, 536, become contemporaries and merge one into another in heroic mythus. But one is hardly prepared to find Dietrich of Bern and Theophilus of Sicily getting confused into one. But so it is. Amongst the Wends it has become a popular story, and is told of Dietrich (Theodoric of Verona), who among the peasantry is transmuted into the Wild Huntsman.

Mr. W. St. Chad Boscawen, in his learned lecture on *A Chaldean Heliopolis*, at Manchester, in December, 1881, after referring to the manner in which Berosus "had resort to an ingenious literary fiction to preserve the continuity of the narrative in his history of Chaldea, which he claimed to have based on documentary evidence, extending back over fifteen myriads of years," says—

The daily recurring war of day and night, which had belonged to the nomadic age, now became national wars and combats of Samson, Shamgar, and Gideon, the solar heroes, against the dark forces of the Philistine and Midianite. But in this period of the heroic age—the 'once upon a time' of the Chaldean story-teller, the nation was not one consolidated whole; it was the age of polyarchy. The beginning of Nimrod's kingdom was not one capital city, it was the tetrapolis of Babel, Akkad, Erech, and Calrech, and each city was a little kingdom. So each city had its hero. The giant Isdubar was the hero of Erech; Sargon the Moses of Chaldea—the hero of Aganne; Etanne and Ner, of Babylon. In the labours and wars of these heroes we saw the labours and wars and struggles of the city kingdom, but lit with the lustre of divinity which shone forth from the age of the gods and clothed with its brightness the characters in the heroic age. But, in time, as the nation became consolidated, all became blended and absorbed into the great national hero, Isdubar, the great king.

The Rev. Sir G. W. Cox, in his *Mythology of the Aryan Nations*, successfully shows that the principal materials of the Arthurian legends are identical with those which underlie the Hindoo, Grecian, Teutonic, and other common Aryan myths. He contends that Arthur is a solar hero, of the same type as Phoibus Chrysâôr, or Heracles, or Bellerophon, or Perseus, or Achilleus, or Sigurd; and he illustrates this position by the citation of numerous instances in which their common original is clearly perceptible, notwithstanding the great modification, especially in costume and morals, to which the original materials have been subjected.

A single instance of this uniformity, but an important one, will suffice for the present purpose. The peculiar form as well as the name of the supernatural weapon of Indra, the Vedic *lightning* god, has undergone many changes in its progress through the mythical lore of the various Aryan nations, and yet its identity is rarely, if ever, doubtful. It is the "Durandal" of Roland; it is Arthur's famous sword "Excalibur," as well as the similar weapon which no one could draw from the "iron anvil-sheaf embedded in stone" except himself. It is the sword of the maiden drawn by Balin, after Arthur had failed in the attempt. It is the "Macabuin," the weapon of the Manx hero, Olave of Norway; it is Odin's sword "Gram," stuck in the roof-tree of Volsung's hall.

It is the sword of Chrysâôr; it is that of Theseus, and that of Sigurd. It is very palpably the spear (Gûngnir) which Odin lent, in the form of a reed, to King Erich, in order to ensure him the victory in a battle against Styrbjörn. The reed in its flight is said to have assumed the form of a spear and *struck with blindness* the whole of the opposing army. It is the arrow with which Apollo slew the Python; it is the lance of St. George, the patron saint of England; it is the "sword of sharpness" of "Jack-the-Giant-Killer;" nay, it is the relatively humble magic cudgel of popular Norse story, which, like Thor's hammer, voluntarily returned to the lad's hand on the completion of the rascally innkeeper's well-merited castigation.

So fascinating are the so-called "historical novels" of such men as Sir Walter Scott and the late Lord Lytton, such "historical plays" as Shakespeare's, and the popular ballads and other lyric narratives of great historical events, that *some* of the most permanent impressions on the mind of the studious, and *many* on that of the relatively non-studious sections of mankind, have been derived therefrom. Indeed, there are persons who roundly assert that "good historical novels" convey to the ordinary reader a better idea of the manners and customs and general aspect of society, as well as of the idiosyncrasies, or special characteristics, of distinguished individuals, than historical works of a more definite and presumedly more reliable character.

Those who entertain these views, however, as a rule, are not themselves historical students in its higher or more legitimate sense, but merely dabblers in history with an æsthetic object. Besides, if the hypothesis be a sound one, these "historical novelists" must themselves be more fully and accurately informed concerning all the hard elements of fact and individual feeling with which they deal than their rivals (which, unfortunately, they never or rarely are), or how could they, by any human process, produce their presumedly more truthful artistic "counterfeit presentments?" The late Lord Lytton, in the preface to the third edition of his novel, Harold, *the last of the Saxon Kings*, expressly says "It was indeed my aim to solve the problem how to produce the greatest amount of *dramatic effect at the least expense of historical truth.*"

On the other hand, Sir Francis Palgrave denounces "historical novels" as the "mortal enemies to history," and Leslie Stephen adds, "they are mortal enemies to fiction" likewise. The latter writer contends, under such conditions, one of two evils necessarily results, notwithstanding the fact that perhaps an isolated exception or two might be cited in opposition:

"Either the novel becomes pure cram, a dictionary of antiquities dissolved in a thin solution of romance, or, which is generally more refreshing, it takes leave of accuracy altogether and simply takes the plot and the costumes from history, but allows us to feel that genuine moderns are masquerading in the dress of a bygone century."

Dean Milman, in his review of Ranke's work on the Papacy, referring to the scene in the conclave on the elevation of Sixtus V. to the Papal chair, which, he says, Gregoria Leti "has drawn with such unscrupulous boldness," adds:

All the minute circumstances of his (the Pope's) manner, speech, and gesture is like one of Scott's happiest historical descriptions, but, we fear, of no better historical authority than the picture of our great novelist.

The false impressions often formed of actual fact from implicit reliance on artistic fiction, as authority in such matters, is admirably illustrated in a passage in *Travels in Central Asia*, by Arminius Vámbéry. After journeying from Tabris to Teheran, he says—

It is a distance of only fifteen, or perhaps we may rather say of only thirteen caravan stations; still, it is fearfully fatiguing, when circumstances compel one to toil slowly from station to station under a scorching sun, mounted upon a laden mule, and condemned to see nothing but such drought and barrenness as characterise almost the whole of Persia. How bitter the disappointment to him who has studied Persia only in Saadi, Khakani, and Hafiz; *or still worse*, who has received his dreamy impressions of the East from the beautiful imaginings of Goethe's *Ost-Westlicher Divan*, or Victor Hugo's *Orientales*, or the magnificent picturings of Tom Moore.

If, under circumstances so favourable as those attendant upon such a *Dryasdust* historical student as Sir Walter Scott, historical truth is violated or perverted as often as it is illustrated, it is painful to reflect what must have resulted when solar and other myths, miraculous legends and traditions of pagan times, have become interwoven with the faith and morals of Christianity, and the pomp and pageantry of medieval chivalry! Leslie Stephens asserts that "*Ivanhoe*, and *Kenilworth*, and *Quentin Durward*, and the rest are, of course, bare, blank impossibilities." "No such people," he declares, "ever lived or talked on this planet." He is willing to allow that some fragments of genuine character may be embedded in what he terms "the plaster of Paris;" but he insists that "there is no solidity or permanence in the workmanship."

If this be true, how has history fared at the hands of such craftsmen as Geoffrey of Monmouth, Archdeacon Walter Map, Sir Thos. Malory, and a whole host of medieval romance writers, with their King Arthur, Sir Lancelot, Sir Galahad, their magicians, sorcerers, giants, dragons, and other monsters? History, in its highest, indeed its only legitimate, sense, most unquestionably has suffered to a much greater extent than can be conceived, except by those who have patiently plodded amongst the details of a portion at least of its dim and dusty, and oft-times doubtful, raw material. But, on the other hand, to the novelist or the poet *historical* truthfulness in the incidents of which his plot is composed, or *biographical* truthfulness in the characters delineated, is simply surplusage, if it be nothing worse, *æsthetic* or artistic verities having no necessary foundation thereupon.

It is this æsthetic ideal, evolved from *general* rather than *individual* truths, this poetic element, which lies at the root, and, indeed, furnishes the *raison d'être*, the very life-giving blood, of such art products as those under consideration. Hamlet, Lear, Imogen, Ophelia, Cordelia, Oberon, Elaine, Sir Galahad, Achilleus, Arthur, *et hoc genus omne*, possess an inherent subjective vitality and truthfulness of their own, drawn from the universal and everlasting fountains of human emotion, passion, and psychical aspiration, however little realistic, individual, or strictly historic value the learned may place on the legends of Saxo Grammaticus and Geoffrey of Monmouth, or the myths of our common Aryan ancestors. Thos. Carlyle, in *Sartor Resartus*, aptly asks— "Was Luther's picture of the devil *less a reality*, whether it were formed within the bodily eye, or without it?"

Dean Milman, in his essay on *Pagan and Christian Sepulchres*, referring to the "two large mounds popularly known as the tombs of the Horatii and the Curiatii," on the Appian way, near Rome, says—

> Let us leave the legend undisturbed, and take no more notice of those wicked disenchanters of our old belief....They will leave us at least the poetry, if they scatter our history into a mist.

Truly the æsthetic element, if in itself worthy, will ever survive the destruction of the presumed historical verity with which it may have been for ages allied. Who now believes in the historic truthfulness of the reputed deeds of the gods and goddesses of ancient Greece and Rome? And yet the æsthetic beauties of Homer, Æschylus, Virgil, and Ovid are none the less admired and enjoyed. Mr. Philip Gilbert Hamerton, in his *Life of J. M. W. Turner*, when commenting on the lack of "topographical," and other realistic truthfulness, both in colour and details, in many of the great landscape painter's finest productions, thus aptly deals with the difference between æsthetic and literal truthfulness—

> It is with these drawings as with the romances of Sir Walter Scott: a time comes in the life of every intelligent reader when he perceives that Scott was not, and could not be, really true to the times he represented, except when they approached very near his own; but a student of literature would be much to be pitied who was unable to enjoy 'Ivanhoe' after this discovery. So when we have found out the excessive freedom which Turner allowed himself; when we have discovered that he is not to be trusted for the representation of any object, however important—that his chiaroscuro, though effective is arbitrary, and his colour though brilliant is false; when we have quite satisfied ourselves, in a word, that he is a poet, and not an architectural draughtsman, or an imitator of nature, is that a reason why we should not enjoy the poems?
>
> There is a wide difference, I grant, between the pleasure of

real belief and the pleasure of confessed imagination: the first belongs to imaginative ignorance, and is only possible for the uncritical; the second belongs to a state of knowledge, and is only possible for those in whom the acquisition of knowledge has not deadened the imaginative faculties. Show the 'Rivers of France' to a boy who has the natural faculties which perceive beauty, but who is still innocent of criticism, he will believe the drawings to be true, and think as he dreams over them that a day may come when he will visit these enchanting scenes. Show them to a real critic, and he will not accept for fact a single statement made by the draughtsman from beginning to end, but he will say—'The poetic power is here,' and then he will yield to its influence, and dream also in his own way—not like the boy, in simple faith, but in the pleasant make-belief faith which is all that the poet asks of us.

This æsthetic truthfulness, in contradistinction to literal historic fact, is admirably expressed by Macaulay in an entry in his journal, in August, 1851. He says—

I walked far into Herefordshire, (from Malvern) and read, while walking, the last five books of the *Iliad*, with deep interest and many tears. I was afraid to be seen crying by the parties of walkers that met me as I came back; crying for Achilles cutting off his hair; crying for Priam rolling on the ground in the courtyard of his house; mere imaginary beings, creatures of an old ballad maker who died near three thousand years ago.

Lord Byron wrote under the influence of the traditions of his youth or of his classical college education, and not as the true poet, when he said—

I stood upon the plain of Troy daily for more than a month, in 1810; and if anything diminished my pleasure it was that the blackguard Bryant had impugned its veracity.

On the contrary, I felt no such lack of pleasurable emotion when I first gazed on the Thames at Datchet, or on the withered trunk of "Herne's Oak," or on the Trossachs and Loch Katrine, or on the Rialto or the Ducal palace at Venice, or on the Colisseum or the adjacent ruins of the "lone mother of dead empires," because the mere *historical* verity of Jack Falstaff's unwieldly carcase, or of Shakespeare, Otway, Byron or Scott's ideal and semi-historical personages, never once entered into my mind. It was sufficient for me that the scenes before me were those which were contemplated and portrayed by the great dramatists and the great novelist and the great poet.

For the time being, thanks to the law of mental association, to my imagination their characters were as real personages as was necessary for the fullest appreciation and enjoyment of the ideal of their artistic creators, and anything more, *being unnecessary*, might have been intrusive, or even *impertinent*, in the original and non-metaphorical meaning of that somewhat abused word. Byron spoke more to the purpose in the opening *stanzas* of the fourth *canto* of *Childe Harold's Pilgrimage*, when, after lamenting the fate of Venice, and recalling the glories of her past history, he exclaims:—

> *But unto us she hath a spell beyond*
> *Her name in story and her long array*
> *Of mighty shadows whose dim forms despond*
> *Above the dogeless city's vanish'd sway;*
> *Ours is a trophy which will not decay*
> *With the Rialto; Shylock and the Moor*
> *And Pierre can not be swept and worn away—*
> *The keystones of the arch! Though all were o'er,*
> *For us repeopled were the solitary shore.*

He adds, with more significant meaning:—

> *The beings of the mind are not of clay;*
> *Essentially immortal, they create*
> *And multiply in us a brighter ray*
> *And more beloved existence.*

Dr. Gervinus says—

Shakespeare's representations of the passionate, the prodigal, the hypocrite, are not portraits of this or that individual, but *examples of those passions elevated out of particular into general truth*, of which, in real life, we may find a thousand diminished copies, but never the original in the exact proportions given by the poet.

And so it is with the æsthetic truth embodied in artistic creations of a plastic or pictorial character. No one acquainted with art products of its class imagines that the colossal statue recently erected in Germany to the memory of Hermann, or Arminius, the conqueror

49

of the Roman legions under Varus (*A.D.* 9), is an absolute every-day portrait-likeness of that not very morally scrupulous "hero and patriot;" or that the faces, figures, costumes, and other accessories, in the "Last Supper" of Da Vinci, or the "Cartoons" of Raffaelle, represent, *historically* or *de facto*, the scenes as they actually occurred. Though conventionally called "historical pictures," they are emphatically creations of the imaginations of the artists, notwithstanding their historic basis, and consequently the great truths that pervade them, and for which they are justly admired, are of an artistic or æsthetic, and not of a strictly historic, character.

Notwithstanding this general lack of historic truthfulness we, nevertheless, do gain valuable knowledge of a psychological, ethnological, and even of a strictly historical character from stories of the mythical and legendary class; but much of that knowledge pertains to the age and its mental associations in which the story-tellers or other artistic exponents themselves lived. In the Arthurian romances we find an immense amount of historic truthfulness with reference to the habits of thought, costume, and religious sentiment, which obtained in and about the twelfth century; but which truths are utterly untrue, as applied by the writers, to the fifth and sixth, the era in which Arthur and his Christian knights, magicians, and giants are presumed to have been corporal existences.

The same may be said of much of Bede's, and, indeed, of most other early chronicles. Although we may refuse our assent to the improbable and miraculous stories therein narrated, we feel convinced, in Bede's instance especially, that the writer is thoroughly in earnest, and honest in his work, and that he, at least, correctly describes the manners, customs, faiths, superstitions, and legendary history prevalent at the period in which he lived. This view is now the one generally accepted by the best historians and ethnological and psychological students. Mr. Ralph N. Wornum, in his *Epochs of Painting Characterised*, says—

Ancient opinions are of themselves facts, and the history of any subject is indeed imperfect when the ideas of early ages regarding it are altogether overlooked, for the impressions and associations made or suggested by any intellectual pursuit are, as one of its effects, a part of the subject itself.

Mr. Tylor, in the work already quoted, says—

"The very myths that were discarded as lying fables prove to be sources of history in ways that their makers and transmitters little dreamed of. Their meaning has been misunderstood, but they have a meaning. Every tale that was ever told has a meaning for the times it belongs to. Even a lie, as the Spanish proverb says, is a lady of birth. ('*La mentira es hija de algo.*') Thus, as evidence of the development of thought as records of long passed belief and usage, even in some measure as materials for the history of the nations owning them, the old myths have fairly taken their place among historic facts; and with such the modern historian, so able and so willing to pull down, is also able and willing to rebuild.

M. Mallet, in his *Northern Antiquities*, referring to the semi-historical romances of the Scandinavians, says—

It is needless to observe that great light may be thrown on the character and sentiments of a nation, by those very books, whence we can learn nothing exact or connected of their history. The most credulous writer, he that has the greatest passion for the marvellous, while he falsifies the history of his contemporaries, paints their manners of life and modes of thinking without perceiving it. His simplicity, his ignorance, are at once pledges of the artless truth of his drawing, and a warning to distrust that of his relations.

Dr. A. Dickson White, in his treatise on *The Warfare of Science*, forcibly illustrates the absolute necessary harmony of all truth, subjective and objective, although we may not always possess sufficient insight to perceive it. He says—

God's truths must agree, whether discovered by looking within upon the soul, or without upon the world. A truth written upon the human heart today, in its full play of emotions or passions, cannot be at any real variance even with a truth written upon a fossil whose poor life ebbed forth millions of years ago.

Professor Gervinus, in his *Shakespeare Commentaries*, has skilfully analysed the distinction between historic and æsthetic truth. He says—

Where the historian, bound by an oath to the severest truth in every single statement, can, at the most, only permit us to divine the causes of events and the motives of actions from the bare narration of facts, the poet, who seeks to draw from these facts only a *general moral truth, and not one of facts*, unites by poetic fiction the action and actors in a distinct living relation of cause and effect. The more freely and boldly he does this, as Shakespeare has done in *Richard III.*, the more poetically interesting will his treatment of the history become, but the more will it lose its historical value; the more truly and closely he adheres to reality, as in *Richard II.*, the more will his poetry gain in historic meaning and forfeit in poetic splendour.

Shakespeare so thoroughly felt and understood this, that in the construction of his plot, and even in the determination of the specialities of the characters of Macbeth and his indomitable wife, he has selected his incidents from more than one epoch in early Scottish history. The famous murder scenes in the first and second acts, so far as they are "historically" true, are drawn from the assassination of a previous king, Duffe, in 971 or 972, by Donwald, captain of the castle of Fores, whose wife is the "historic" original of the "æsthetic" Lady Macbeth of the tragedy, and not the spouse (if he had one) of the chieftain who, history simply says, "slew the king (Duncan) at Inverness," in an ordinary battle in 1040.

Professor Gervinus adds—

It is a common pride on the part of the poets of these historical plays, and a natural peculiarity belonging to this branch of the art, that truth and poetry should go hand in hand. It is more than probable that *Henry VIII.* bore at first the title so characteristic in this respect—*All is True*. But this truth is throughout, as we have seen, not to be taken in the prosaic sense of the historian, who seeks it in the historical material in every most minute particular, and in its most different aspects; it is only a higher and universal truth which is gathered by a poet from a series of historical facts, yet which from the very circumstance that it springs from historical, true and actual facts, and is supported and held by them, acquires, it must be admitted, a double authority, that of poetry and history combined. The historical drama, formed of these two component parts, is therefore especially agreeable to the imaginative friend of history and the realistic friend of poetry.

It will thus be seen that there is no necessary antagonism between individual, or historic, and ideal, or æsthetic, truth. Their respective lines of action may be divergent, but they are, when thoroughly understood, both in harmony with the great central and "eternal verity" which embodies all truth. The only danger to be guarded against by the historic or æsthetic student arises from the too common habit of confounding the one with the other.

Tennyson, in his *Queen Mary*, says—

The very Truth and very Word are one,
But truth of story, which I glanced at, girl,
Is like a word that comes from olden days,
And passes thro' the peoples: every tongue
Alters it passing, till it spells and speaks
Quite other than at first.

Nennius speaks of a tenth battle fought and won by Arthur on the banks of the river Trat Treuroit, or Ribroit. This has been identified by commentators as the Brue, in Somersetshire, and the Ribble, in Lancashire; but the evidence advanced is not very conclusive in favour of either locality. Mr. Haigh prefers Trefdraeth, in the island of Anglesea, as the place indicated.

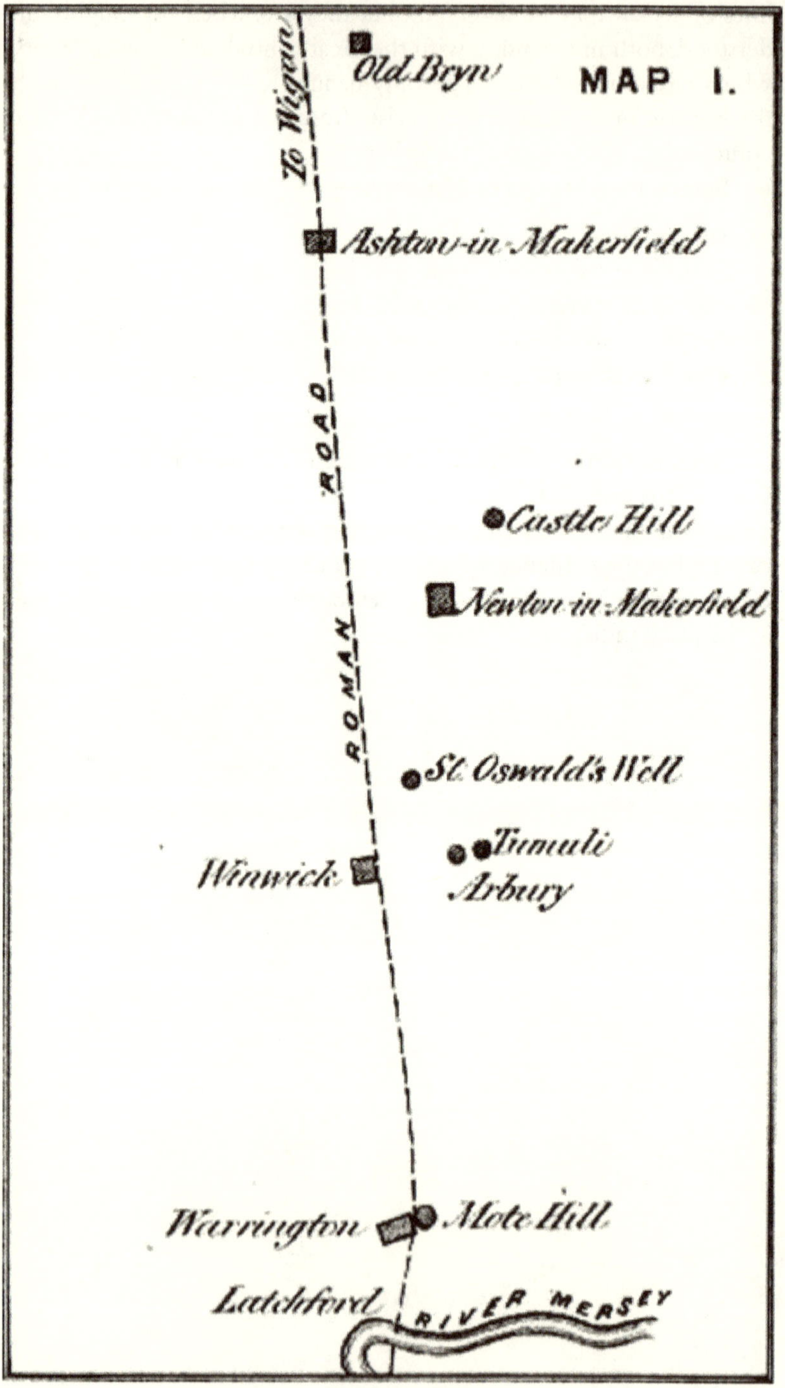

MAP I.

Old Bryn

To Wigan

Ashton-in-Makerfield

ROMAN ROAD

Castle Hill

Newton-in-Makerfield

St. Oswald's Well

Winwick

Tumuli
Arbury

Warrington   Mote Hill

Latchford   RIVER MERSEY

Chapter 2

The Defeat and Death of St. Oswald, of Northumbria, at Maserfeld, (A.D. 642)

The Venerable Bede, in the ninth chapter of his *Ecclesiastical History of the English Nation*, says, in the year 642—

Oswald was killed in a great battle, by the same Pagan nation and Pagan king of the Mercians who had slain his predecessor, Edwin, at a place called in the English tongue, Maserfelth, in the thirty-eighth year of his age, on the fifth day of the month of August.

The *Anglo-Saxon Chronicle*, under the same date, says—

This year Oswald, King of the Northumbrians, was slain by Penda and the South-humbrians at Maserfeld, on the *nones* of August, and his body was buried at Bardney (Lincolnshire). His sanctity and miracles were afterwards manifested in various ways beyond this island, and his hands are at Bamborough (Northumberland), uncorrupted.

The battle is likewise recorded by relatively more recent chroniclers, yet its site, hitherto, has not been satisfactorily determined. Camden, Capgrave, Pennant, Sharon-Turner, and some others fix it at Oswestry, in Shropshire; while Archbishop Usher, Alban Butler, Powell, Dr. Cowper, Edward Baines, Thomas Baines, W. Beaumont, Dr. Kendrick, Mr. T. Littler, and others prefer the neighbourhood of Winwick, in the "Fee of Makerfield," Lancashire.[1]

---

1. Dean Howson, in an address delivered at Chester, in 1873, (continued next page)

Mr. Edward Baines says—

The district in which Winwick is seated has, from a very distant period, been denominated Mackerfield or Macerfield—a battlefield, with variations in the orthography usually found in Norman and Anglo-Saxon writers." The late Rev. Edmund Simpson, vicar of Ashton-in-Mackerfield, however, disputes this etymology, and contends that "Mackerfield is Mag-er-feld, a great plain cultivated: *mag* and *er* being Gaelic and *feld* Saxon. Thus Maghull, near Liverpool, is a hill on the plain: thus, also, Maghera-felt in Ireland.

The "Fee of Makerfield" was co-extensive with the Newton hundred of the Domesday record, and included nineteen townships. It extended from Wigan to Winwick, and was traversed in its entire length by the great Roman road, which entered Northumbria from the south near Warrington.

Professor Dwight Whitney, in his *Life and Growth of Language*, says—

Æcer meant in Anglo-Saxon a 'cultivated field,' as does the German *acker* to the present day; and here, again, we have its very ancient correlatives in Sanscrit *agra*, Greek ἀγρός, , Latin *ager*; the restriction of the word to signify a field of certain fixed dimensions, taken as a unit of measure for fields in general, is something quite peculiar and recent. It is analagous with the like treatment of *rod* and *foot* and *grain*, and so on, except that in these cases we have saved the old meaning while adding the new.

Field is from A.S., O.S., and Ger. *feld*, Danish *veld*, the open *country*, cleared lawn (*Collins's Dic. Der.*) With respect to acre the old meaning is still retained, in one instance at least. We still say "God's acre," when

in reference to the disputed site of Oswald's death, said—"He was not going to decide between the claims of the two places, but he was inclined to think both views might be reconciled. Oswald had a palace at Winwick, and there was a well there that bore his name, and an inscription that recorded his attachment to the locality. Oswestry was said to mean Oswald's tree. There was no reason why they should not believe that he was killed at Winwick, and that his head and arms were taken away and put on a stump of wood at Oswestry. The conflicting statements would then be reconciled." Such an act would, in no way, be inconsistent with the character of Penda. He might send the remains to his Welsh allies as trophies of his victory over the vanquisher of their great chief, Cadwalla.

speaking of a churchyard or burial ground.

The following are some of the principal variations in the writing of the name: Bede calls it Maserfelth, King Alfred writes it Maserfeld, as in one MS. of the *Anglo-Saxon Chronicle*. Another copy, however, has it Maresfeld. The latter is probably a clerical error resultant from the accidental misplacement of the letters *r* and *s* by the copyist, or it may be an ordinary example of what philologists call "metathesis," or transliteration. Matthew of Westminster writes it Marelfeld, and John of Brompton, Maxelfeld. Matthew and John, however, are relatively modern authorities in comparison with Bede, the Anglo-Saxon Chronicle, and Alfred. Their orthography, however, furnishes an apt illustration of the mutation which has taken place in local nomenclature during the transition of the language from Anglo-Saxon to modern English, and hence the occasional difficulty of satisfactory identification at the present day.

The phonetic difficulty between Maserfeld, Macerfeld, and Makerfield is, perhaps, not insurmountable. The letter *c* in English is useless, having either the sound of *k* or *s*. Before *a*, *o*, and *u*, it becomes *k*, as in cat, cot, cure; before *e* and *i* it becomes *s*, as in century, certain, cinder, and city. Cer, likewise, by metathesis, or the transposition of the *r*, becomes cre, as in lucre, massacre, etc. Thus it would appear the modern word "Makerfield" probably accords both etymologically and topographically with the Anglo-Saxon name of the site of the battle. As no other hamlet, township, or parish, or other territorial designation[2] (the nearest being Macclesfield), does this, especially when taken

---

2. The etymology on which Mr. Howel W. Lloyd, the recent able advocate for the Shropshire site, and others, rely, (Earwaker's *Local Gatherings relating to Lancashire*, vol. i., 1876, and the summary, by Mr. Askew Roberts, in his *Contributions to Oswestry History*,) is as follows:—Referring to Mr. Lloyd's paper, Mr. Roberts states his position thus:—"Mesbury (now Maesbury, called in Domesday Meresbury), a hamlet in the parish of Oswestry, is now called 'Llysfeisir or Llys feisydd.'" He adds—"Thus a basis is supplied for a correct inference as to the order of nomenclature. 1. The Welsh Te-fesen, corrupted by the Saxons into Mesafelth or Maserfelth, and then into Maserfield, the name of the district in which is Oswestry, as Winwick is in Makerfield. 2. The monastery founded on the spot in honour of St. Oswald, called Album Monasterium, Candida Ecclesia Y Fonachlog Wen (by the Welsh according to Davies), and Blancmonster and Blancminster by the Normans, all meaning the same thing, viz.:—White Monastery, applied latterly also to the town, which grew up around the monastery. 3. Mesbury, corrupted into Maesbury, when the town in Trefesen, to which a Fitzalan granted a charter, grew into a borough; and 4, Oswaldestree or Oswestry, from the 'tre' or district, or else possibly from the traditional tree, on which the king's arm was recorded to have been hung. (Continued next page).,

57

in conjunction with the many corroborative evidences, would appear to satisfactorily identify the locality.[3] These corroborative evidences are by no means either scanty or unimportant.

The parish church of Winwick is dedicated to St. Oswald, and Mr. Baines says—

> Little more than half a mile to the north, on the road to Golborne and Wigan, is an ancient well, which has been known from time immemorial by the name of 'St. Oswald's Well.'

This well is still in existence, and a certain veneration at the present time hovers about it in the minds of others than the superstitious peasantry. On the upper portion of the south wall of the church is an inscription in Latin, purporting to be a "renovation" of a previous one, by a person named Sclater, in the year 1530, in the curacy of Henry Johnson. On a recent visit, this inscription, as well as other portions of the edifice, I found had undergone further renovation. Gough translates the first three lines as follows:—

> *This place of old did Oswald greatly love:*
> *Who the Northumbers ruled, now reigns above,*
> *And from Marcelde did to Heaven remove.*

Mr. Beamont gives the translation of the inscription as follows:—

> *This place of yore did Oswald greatly love,*

A further basis is supplied for reconciling the statement of Nennius, that the battle was fought at Codoy, with that of the Saxon historian that it was fought at Maserfield. For just as Winwick is in Mackerfield, so may Codoy have been in the larger locality of Maserfield; and Nennius, as a British historian, representing, as his editors believe him to do, a much earlier author, gives, as might naturally be expected, the precise situation of the spot, the territorial appellation only for which reached the foreign and more distant chroniclers. From all this it is certain that Oswestry had its Maserfield as Winwick its Mackerfield, the former, however, more nearly reflecting the ancient British name, as well as character of the place, but both alike designating a district rather than a town, that being the ancient meaning of the word 'tre.' Maserfelth is, therefore, Oak-field, a translation of the original British name of Trefesen (compare English 'mast,') and the arms connected St. Oswald with the Oak."

3. Bosworth, in his Anglo-Saxon dictionary, under the letter K, says, "Though the A. S. generally used *c*, even before *e, i*, and *y*, yet as *k* is sometimes found," he gives a list of words commencing with that consonant under such conditions. The Anglo-Saxon "Cymen's ora" is now represented by Keynor. Kemble says the homes of the Elsingas and Elcinghas, are now represented by Elsing and Elkington, in Northamptonshire. Mr. Green speaks of "those Gewissas, the Hwiccas, as they were called," and Peille says, "Indo-European *ky* and *ty* become*ss*, as in 'prasso' for 'prack-yo' (root 'prack,' formative suffix 'yo.')"

Northumbria's King, but now a saint above,
Who in Marcelde's field did fighting fall,
Hear us, oh blest one, when here to thee we call.
(A line over the porch obliterated.)
In fifteen hundred and just three times ten,
Sclater restored and built this wall again,
And Henry Johnson here was curate then.

This, and its repetition by Hollingworth in his *Mancuniensis*, appears to have alone constituted "the highest authority" relied upon by Edward Baines for his statement that Winwick parish was the favourite residence of King Oswald. The inscription does not, as some have assumed, state the church is built in, on, or near Marcelde. It merely asserts that Oswald died at a place so named, and which may have been Winwick, the site of the church dedicated to St. Oswald, or any other locality, Marcelde being evidently a corruption and a rythmical contraction of the undoubted Anglo-Saxon name of the scene of Oswald's defeat and death.

Objection has been taken to the word "*Marcelde,*" as a bad Latin substitute for "Maserfeld." But the goodness or badness of medieval Latin substitutes for English names is of no consequence to the question at issue, as the reference to the place of Oswald's death is undeniable. It is but an apt illustration of the strange transformations local nomenclature sometimes has undergone in transmission from past centuries to the present time.

Geoffrey of Monmouth and the Welsh Bruts curiously confound the incidents attendant upon this and a previous battle, in which Oswald was engaged and was victorious. Geoffrey says that Cadwalla, a Brit-Welsh king, one of the heroes of Lywrich Hen's poetic effusions, *hearing of Oswald's victory over Penda(?)* at "Heavenfield," "being inflamed with rage, assembled his army and went in pursuit of the holy king, Oswald; and in a battle which he had with him, at a place called Burne, broke in upon him and killed him."

Geoffrey here, as noted by Sharon-Turner, shows his irrational partiality to the fame of the British chieftain, and his disregard of historical truth when it did not minister to his prejudices or presumed patriotism. Cadwalla was slain in the battle with Oswald at "Heavenfield," in 635, seven years previously to the saintly Northumbrian warrior's defeat and death; and, consequently, the British hero was, in accordance with ordinary mortal notions, somewhat incapacitated for the performance of the after-deeds of valour, ascribed to him by his panegyrist—without miraculous intervention—which, however, Geoffrey does not even suggest, notwithstanding its presumed frequency on other momentous occasions.[4]

Referring to Oswald's death, Bede says—

> It is also given out and become a proverb, 'that he ended his life in prayer;' for when he was beset with weapons and enemies, he perceived he must immediately be killed, and prayed to God for the souls of his army, hence it is proverbially said, 'Lord have mercy on their souls, said Oswald, as he fell on the ground.' His bones, therefore, were translated to the monastery which we mentioned (Bardsea), and buried therein; but the king that slew him commanded his head, hands, and arms to be cut off from the body, and set upon stakes. But the successor in the throne, Oswy, coming thither the next year with his army, took them down, and buried his head in the church of Lindisfarne, and the hands and arms in the royal city" (Bamborough).

Bede relates many anecdotes, illustrative of the sanctity of Oswald, and the miracles wrought by his bones, as well as by the earth which received his blood on the battlefield. One instance I give entire, in Dr. Giles's translation of the venerable historian's own words. In chapter x., book iii., he says—

> About the same time, another person of the British nation, *as is reported*, happened to travel by the same place, where the aforesaid battle was fought, and observing one particular spot of ground, green and more beautiful than any other part of the field, he judiciously concluded with himself that there could be no other cause for that unusual greenness but that some person of more holiness than any other in the army had been killed there. He therefore took along with him some of that earth, tying it up in a linen cloth, supposing it would some time or other be of use for curing sick people, and proceeding on

---

4. There is great difficulty in reconciling the various statements respecting this Cadwalla. Mr. Skene (*Four Ancient Books of Wales*) thinks it not improbable that it was his father, Cadvan, who fell at Heavenfield, and not himself. If Cadwalla fought at Maserfeld, Dean Howson's conjecture is rendered more probable. See *Ante.* Revenge for his father's death might induce him to display his trophies of victory over his previously successful rival before his Brit-Welsh subjects at a locality afterwards named Oswestry..

his journey, he came at night to a certain village, and entered a house where the neighbours were feasting at supper; being received by the owners of the house, he sat down with them at the entertainment, hanging the cloth in which he had brought the earth, on a post against the wall.

They sat long at supper and drank hard, with a great fire in the middle of the room; it happened that the sparks flew up and caught the top of the house, which being made of wattles and thatch, was presently in a flame; the guests ran out in a fright, without being able to put a stop to the fire. The house was consequently burnt down, only that post on which the earth hung remained entire and untouched. On observing this, they were all amazed, and inquiring into it diligently, understood that the earth had been taken from the place where the blood of King Oswald had been shed. These miracles being made known and reported abroad, many began daily to frequent that place, and received health to themselves and theirs.

In June, 1856, whilst I was engaged superintending the excavations at "Castle Hill," Penwortham, near Preston, an incident occurred, which, "in the olden time," would have been regarded as a conclusive proof not only of the miraculous quality of the earth on which St. Oswald expired, but of the site of the battlefield. We found, under the mound excavated, the remains of an edifice which had been destroyed apparently partly by fire, and on the ruins of which to the height of about 12 or 14 feet, the Anglo-Saxon *tumulus* had been piled. The hill, situated at the nose of the promontory overlooking the upper portion of the Ribble estuary, had evidently been occupied at one time as a *specula*, or outpost, in connection with the Roman station at Walton-le-dale. The wattle and thatch characteristics of the remains of the fallen roof of the edifice were very apparent.

But the most remarkable, nay, inexplicable feature disclosed, was a single oak pillar, with wooden peg-holes in it, standing erect near the centre of the mound, while the remainder of the structure was scattered in confusion on a mass of debris and vegetable litter, in which were found, together with several articles in metal, etc., an enormous quantity of bones of animals, evidently killed and eaten for food. To the persistent enquiries of several somewhat bewildered persons, anxious to discover an *immediate* explanation of so remarkable a fact, I at length yielded, and related, in a serious, but not *authoritative* manner, the statement of Bede,

61

and I feel confident several persons returned home with a conviction that the story was probable enough, or at least there was something either miraculous or "uncanny" about the whole affair.

Without, of course, assenting to the miraculous medicinal quality of the earth, it is highly improbable that so conscientious, if credulous, a writer as Bede would relate such a story, unless there had been some substratum of *prosaic fact reported to him*, on which the miraculous element might easily have been engrafted in those superstitious days. It is not improbable that the accidental preservation of the pillar to which was hung the presumed sacred earth on which the saintly monarch breathed his last, prevented its destruction or removal, and hence its position near the centre of the mound raised above the ruined edifice, and, doubtless, afterwards used as a "mote hill," or out-of-door justice seat, or place of public assembly. If Winwick be the site of the battlefield, the traveller passing from thence northward by the great Roman road would arrive at Penwortham in time for supper, presuming that his journey commenced three or four hours previously.

All this may not be worth much more than some of the idle tales of the old "historians" in support of the claims of the Lancashire site as the locality of the great battle between the Christian and Pagan elements in the population of the northern portion of England in the seventh century.[5] Nevertheless, it presents, at least, one of those remarkable coincidences that occasionally puzzle our reason and perplex our faith. Deeper insight into the psychological aspect of the humanity of any period may often be gained by a careful study of their legendary lore and cherished superstitions than from the perusal of the more orthodox historical chronicles. But there are other evidences respecting the site of this important Anglo-Saxon conflict, more reliable than the miracles of tradition, which demand our attention.

From the antecedents of the respective belligerents, and the statement of Bede, it seems almost certain that the Pagan chieftain, Penda, was the aggressor, and, anxious to avenge the death of Cadwalla, his *quasi*-Christian ally, invaded the Northumbrian kingdom, on the frontier of which he was successfully confronted by his Christian antagonist. The tradition in Geoffrey's day, at least, distinctly states that Oswald's conqueror was the aggressor. He says—"inflamed with rage, he went in pursuit of the holy king." See *Ante*.

---

5. Mr. Hartshorne, however, refers to this story in connection with his claim of "Maesbrook, a place in a direct line between Maesbury and Coedway, and about five miles from Oswestry," as the site of Oswald's defeat, and connects a local legend with it.

Referring to the antecedents of the war under Oswy, which followed Oswald's death, and in which Penda was slain near the river Winwid, Mr. Green (*Making of England*) says—

That Oswiu strove to avert the conflict we see from the delivery of his youngest son, Ecgfrith, as a hostage into Penda's hands. The sacrifice, however, proved useless. Penda was *again the assailant*, and his attack was as vigorous as of old.

We, therefore, in the first instance, should naturally look for the battlefield in Northumbria, rather than in North Wales,[6] or even in Mercia.

Another important element with reference to the disputed site has not hitherto, to my knowledge, received the attention it deserves. Geoffrey of Monmouth, and the Welsh Bruts, notwithstanding their determination to give all the honour to the defunct British chief, Cadwalla, could have no motive for falsifying the site of the battle. Indeed, his reference to it by name, as will be seen by the extract previously given, is of an ordinary passing character.

Now, there is a locality, in the parish of Winwick, and in the "Fee of Makerfield," to the north of the great barrow or tumulus, to which I shall call further attention, that answers, on true phonetic laws, to this nomenclature. Mr. Edward Baines says—

The original proprietors of the township of Ashton (which is the largest township in the old parish of Winwick) derived their name from Bryn Hall, the place of their residence, or gave their name to that place, and Alan le Brun occurs in the *Testa de Nevill*, as holding by ancient tenure two bovates of land for 6s. of Sir Henry de Le.

It is here apparent that the present name Bryn was originally Brun, and, as brun and burn are, by what philologists term transliteration, but different renderings of the same word, meaning a spring or brook, Geoffrey's varied reading of the name of the locality—"at a place called *Burne*," strongly supports the other evidence in favour of the Lancashire site. Edward Baines, referring to the ancient Lancashire family, the Gerards of Bryn, says—

This family have had four seats within the township of Ashton, (in Makerfield), namely, Old Bryn, abandoned five centuries

---

6. For a long time after the death of Oswald, the present Shropshire remained British, or as Professor Boyd Dawkins appropriately terms it, "Brit-Welsh," territory.— See Mr. Green's maps.

ago; New Bryn, erected in the reign of Edward VI.; Garswood, taken down at the beginning of the present century; and the new hall, the present residence of the family.

Nennius says Penda slew Oswald at the "Battle of Cocboy,"[7] and that "he gained the victory by diabolical agency." No attempt, however, within my knowledge, has been made to identify "Cocboy" with any existing locality. There is, however, I understand, a place near the ancient pass of the Mersey, or Latchford, and contiguous to the great Roman road, named Cockedge. As Cocboy is unknown this may be a corruption of it. Etymologists identify *coc* with the British *gosh* or red. As the new red sandstone crops out in the neighbourhood, this interpretation accords with the local condition.

Latchford, too, would be significant, if like *Lich*field, it had its root in the Anglo-Saxon *lic*, but this is doubtful. Lichfield or Litch-field, the "field of dead bodies," is said to have derived its name from the circumstance that "many suffered martyrdom there in the time of Dioclesian."[8] In Gibson's *Etymological Geography*, *Win*-feld, where Arminius, or Hermann, defeated the Roman legions under Varus, A.D. 10, is said to signify the "field of victory." A similar etymology is equally valid for *Win*wick, and hence its significance. Indeed, the intransitive form of the Anglo-Saxon verb *winnan*, whence our *win*, signifies "To gain the victory." A similar interpretation will equally apply to Winwidfield, near Leeds, the scene of Penda's subsequent defeat and death.

When dealing with the identification of modern with ancient names, it is well to bear in mind the remarks of so erudite a philologist as Professor Dwight Whitney. In his *Life and Growth of Language*, he says—

---

7. The Welsh authorities write this word "Codoy." The Rev. W. Gunn and Dr. Giles, "Cocboy."

8. The martyrdom is a very doubtful matter; indeed, it is more than probable this name of the field, and its presumed etymology, gave birth to the legend, or it may have been an ancient burial place. A Lancashire peasant pronounces the word neither, nather and nother, at the present day, while some clergymen pronounce it nigh-ther. The Lancashire contraction for James is Jim not Jem, as in the South of England. I have often heard China pronounced "Chaney" by Lancashire people. The number of ancient burial tumuli to the north of the ford may possibly have influenced the local nomenclature. In Webster's dictionary a third meaning to the word "latch" is thus described: "3. [Fr. lécher, to lick, pour. O. H. Ger. *lecchôn*. See Lick.] To smear [Obs.]"

It must be carefully noted, indeed, that the reach of phonetics, its power to penetrate to the heart of its facts and account for them, is only limited. There is always one element in linguistic change which refuses scientific treatment, namely, the action of the human will. The work is all done by human beings, adapting means to ends, under the impulse of motives and the guidance of habits which are the resultant of causes so multifarious and obscure that they elude recognition and defy estimate.

Every period of linguistic life, with its constantly progressive changes of form and meaning, wipes out a part of the intermediates which connect a derived element with its original. There are plenty of items of word-formation in even the modern Romanic languages, which completely elude explanation. Mere absence of evidence, then, will not in the least justify us in assuming the genesis of an obscure form to be of a wholly different character from that which is obvious or demonstrable in other forms. The presumption is wholly in favour of the accordance of the one with the other; it can only be repelled by direct and convincing evidence.

As linguistics is a historical science, so its evidences are historical, and its methods of proof of the same character. There is no absolute demonstration about it: *there is only probability*, in the same varying degree as elsewhere in historical enquiry. There are no rules, the strict application of which will lead to infallible results. Nothing will make dispensable the wide gathering-in of evidence, the careful sifting of it, so as to determine what bears upon the case in hand and how directly, the judicial balancing of apparently conflicting testimony, the refraining from pushing conclusions beyond what the evidences warrant, the willingness to rest, when necessary, in a merely negative conclusion, which should characterize the historical investigator in all departments.

The most important ancient structure at present remaining in the parish of Winwick is an immense *tumulus* called "Castle Hill." Mr. Edward Baines says—

At the distance of half-a-mile from and to the north of Newton, stands an ancient barrow, called *Castle Hill*. It is romantically situated on elevated ground, at the junction of two streams, whose united waters form the brook which flows past the lower part of the town of Newton.[9] The sides and summit of the barrow are covered with venerable oaks, which to all appearance have weathered the rude and wintry blasts for centuries. It is a spot well adapted for the repose of the ashes of the mighty dead.

Mr. W. Beamont, in a paper read before the Lancashire and Cheshire Historic Society, on the "Fee of Makerfield," etc., in March, 1873, says,—

On the west side of this rivulet (the Golbourne brook), where the red rock rises above it, there is scooped out a rude alcove or cave, which the country people assign to Robin Hood, the popular hero, who in most of our northern counties divides with Arthur of the Round Table and Alfred the Great the right to legendary fame. The Castle Hill, which stands in a commanding position above the other bank of the stream, and is boul-shaped, is 320 feet in circumference at the base, 226 feet in circumference at the top, and it has an elevation of 17 feet above the level of the field below.

On a recent visit I found the old oaks, like faithful veteran sentinels, still guarding, in Mr. Baines's language, "the repose of the mighty dead." One or two of them, however, exhibited unmistakeable evidence that the rude blast of the storm-wind and fiery embrace of the lightning-flash had shattered their aged limbs, while the benumbing grasp of Time had chilled their heretofore invigorating sap. Yet, although they are destined, in a relatively very short period, from *their* chronological standpoint, to succumb to the destiny of all organic life, and finish their lengthened existence in ignominious association with the faggot-shed, still their venerable forms, notwithstanding the dilapidations which attest the force of years of elemental conflict, in conjunction with the historic and legendary memories with which they are associated, render them more suggestive teachers in their decay than they were in the pride of their stalwart and umbrageous prime.

Another change has likewise come over the scene since Mr. Beamont's description was written. The stream near Newton has been blocked by an earthen embankment, and the "Castle Hill" now overlooks a beautiful artificial lake, with three branches. Robin Hood's cave, alas! had to be sacrificed; four or five feet of water now placidly flows over the site of its former entrance.

---

9. The Rev. E. Sibson says—"The streams which unite at this barrow are the Dene and the Sankey." Mr. Beamont says the *tumulus* is situated on the Golbourne brook.

This *tumulus*, situated on the Gol-*bourne* brook, in the Fee of Mackerfield, was opened on the 8th of July, 1843. An account of this excavation, by the Rev. E. Sibson, was published in the *Transactions of the Manchester Literary and Philosophical Society* at the time, from which I gather the following important particulars. Mr. W. Beamont, who was present during the excavations, likewise (in the paper previously quoted) gives a detailed account of the mode of procedure adopted, and of the remains discovered. The mound was found to be artificial, and composed of earth, sand, and rock taken from a trench on the south and west sides. This trench was then found to be about five feet deep and forty feet wide. It appeared to have been originally seven feet deep, two of which had been excavated out of the solid rock. A shaft six feet wide was sunk in the centre of the tumulus, and an adit to meet it, from the west side, on the level of the original soil. Mr. Beamont says—

At the distance of about ten feet from the centre of the barrow, on the south side of the shaft, a chamber was discovered. The base of this chamber was two feet broad, and it was curved. Its length was twenty-one feet, its height two feet, and the roof was a semi-circular arch. It seemed to be constructed of masses of clay, about a foot in diameter, rolled into form in a moist state, and closely compacted by pressure. When the chamber was first opened the candles were extinguished, and there was great difficulty in breathing. The sides and bottom of the chamber were coated with impalpable powder, of smoke colour.

The bottom of the chamber was covered with a dark-coloured substance. The external surface of this substance was like peat earth, being rough, uneven, and of a black colour. The inside of it, when broken, was close and compact, and somewhat similar to black sealing-wax, which, when examined by the microscope, was found to be closely dotted with particles of lime. It was thought to be a mixture of wood ashes, half burned animal matter, and calcined bones. On this plate of animal matter, which had been placed on the edge of the original green sward, was a covering of loose earth, about two inches in thickness, which might have fallen from the roof and sides of the chamber.

Immediately below the plate of animal matter a trench had been cut, about fifteen inches deep, and two tiers of round oak timber had been placed in it. The first tier was notched into the green sward, and the second tier was nine inches below it. The horizontal distance of the several pieces was about eighteen inches, and the pieces in the lower tier were placed exactly opposite to those in the upper one. Several of the pieces were charred, and many of them had entirely disappeared, leaving black marks in the sides of the trench, where they had formerly been placed. These pieces of oak appeared to have been three or four inches in diameter.

In almost all the cases the wood of these pieces had been absorbed; in some cases the bark on the underside of these pieces was carbonised, and had nearly the appearance of coal; and in other cases the bark on the underside of these pieces retained its original form and colour. In one case, however, one of these pieces, in contact with the animal matter, had the appearance of dry decayed wood. The trench, below the plate of animal matter, was filled with clay.

Mr. Beamont gives several other interesting details, and adds,—

It is probable that this chamber contained the original deposit, and that it had never been opened before. On the roof of the east side of the chamber there was discovered a very distinct and remarkable impression of a human body. There was the cavity formed by the back of the head, and this cavity was coated with a very thin shell of carbonised matter. The depression of the back of the neck, the projection of the shoulders, the elevation of the spine, and the protuberance of the lower part of the body, were distinctly visible. The body had been that of an adult, and the head lay towards the west. The exact form and vertical position of the circular chamber was indicated by a ridge on the crest of the hill, which was one reason why the tunnel was driven from the bottom of the shaft towards the south.

The writer further informs us that the "Castle Hill is said to be haunted by a white lady, who flits and glides, but never walks. She is sometimes seen at midnight, but is never heard to speak." The Rev. Mr. Sibson adds—"There is a tradition that Alfred the Great was buried here, with a crown of gold, in a silver coffin." He likewise says that:

In a drift, on the east side of the shaft, and near the centre of the hill, a broken whetstone was found. It was of freestone of a fine grain, of a dull white colour, slightly veined with red; and the surface was finely polished. It was about five inches in length and three in breadth.

He likewise figures a fragment of an urn, apparently of Roman manufacture, from the presence of which he inferred that "the Castle Hill had been a place of interment for persons of distinction for a long period."

Dr. James Fergusson, in an appendix to his work on *Rude Stone Monuments of All Countries,* gives, at length, an account of the opening, in 1846, of a huge *tumulus,* named "Oden's Howe," near Upsala, by Herr Hildebrand, the royal antiquary of Sweden. The similarity of many of the remains brought to light to those found in the "Castle Hill," seems to suggest that these *tumuli* were erected by cognate people, and at no very distant periods from each other. Herr Hildebrand says,—

> During the diggings were found unburnt animal bones, bits of dark wood, charcoal, bits of burnt bones, etc. This was evidently a sepulchral mound. Diggings have also been made in the smaller cairns nearby, and, although they have been opened before, burial urns have been found, burnt human bones, bones of animals and birds, bits of iron and bronze, etc. . . . At the middle of the howe, the grave-chamber is nine feet above the level of the soil, 18 feet under the top of the howe. On the bed of the clay, under the great stones, have been found an iron clinker three inches long, remains of pine poles partly burnt, a lock of hair chestnut coloured, etc. The numerous clusters of charcoal show that the dead had been burned on the layer of clay, and the bones have been collected in an urn not yet found. In one of the nearest small howes have been found a quantity of burnt animal and human bones, two little-injured bronze brooches, a fragment of a golden ornament, etc."

After further examination of the contents of the howe, Herr Hildebrand says:

> *June 29th, 1847,*—The burial urn has been found in the grave-chamber, also have turned up bones of men, horses, dogs, a golden ornament delicately worked, a bone comb, bone buttons, etc.

He afterwards writes to say that the burial urn was found three

69

inches under the soil, and was covered with a thin slab.

It was seven inches high, nine inches in diameter, filled with burnt bones, human and animal (horse, dog, etc.), ashes, charcoal (of needle and leaf trees), nails, copper ornaments, bone articles, a bird of bone, etc. In the mass of charcoal also were found bones, broken ornaments, bits of two golden bracteates, etc. Coins of King Oscar were then placed in the urn, and everything restored as before. Frey's Howe was opened, and showed the same results.

Dr. Fergusson, commenting on this, says—

With a little local industry, I have very little doubt, not only that the date of these tombs could be ascertained, but the names of the royal personages who were therein buried, probably in the sixth or seventh century of our era.

In a paper read before the Lancashire and Cheshire Historic Society, in March, 1860, the late Dr. Robson says—

In the Ordnance survey as first published on the inch scale, about half a mile to the east of Winwick church, we find a couple of tumuli, one on each side of a bye-lane; but in the later and larger map, a single tumulus is marked, through the centre of which the road seems to have been cut. The earlier survey gives the more correct representation of the place, as there have certainly been at least two barrows, one in the field on the east, the other in that of the west side of the lane.

The latter is on a farm called "Highfields." As the land has long been under cultivation, the *tumulus* was not very well defined, but it appeared to have been about thirty yards in diameter. The summit is "distinct enough," says Dr. Robson, and "is about six feet above the level of the lane." This mound was dug into in November, 1859, and the Dr. records that:

Deposits of burned bones were found at some distance from its centre, on the slopes to the east and south. These bones were in small fragments, apparently in distinct heaps, mixed with minute particles of burnt wood, and one or two fragments of brown, thick, ill-burnt and rude pottery turned up, not, however, appearing to have any connection with the bone deposits—the only portion of which offering any recognisable character, was the head of a

70

thigh bone of a subject twelve or fourteen years old. About six feet deep in the centre, the red sandstone rock was reached. . . . Some labourers working in the field on the other side of the lane, fifteen years ago, came upon an urn with bones in it, apparently of a similar description. This *tumulus* was removed at the beginning of the present year, and the men in their operations cutting into some soft black stuff, struck a spade into an urn and broke it into pieces; it seems to have been of large size, and has a feathered pattern scored on the outside, in other respects agreeing with the fragments already described. It contained bones in the same fragmentary state as those found on the west side of the lane, and with them a stone hammer-head and a bronze dart.

Near these *tumuli*, on the ordnance map, is a place named Arbury. This name has evidently had originally some connection with these mounds. In the *Imperial Gazetteer*, Arbury, in Herts, on the Icknield-st., is described as a "Roman camp," and so is Arbury or Harborough, near Cambridge, as well as Arbury Banks, on the Watling-st., near Chipping Norton, Northamptonshire. In Anglo-Saxon the prefix *ar*, according to Bosworth's Dictionary, signifies "glory, honour, respect, reverence," etc.

Dr. Robson discusses at some length the presumed date of these interments, and contends that such nomenclature as "stone and bronze periods" only mislead. He says—

In some graves are coins which carry a date with them, and in others Roman remains which belong to the first four centuries of our era. But in *tumuli* such as those at Winwick, there is nothing to show whether it was raised six centuries before or six centuries after that period.

From the drawings which accompany Dr. Robson's paper, there appears nothing to vitiate the hypothesis that these mounds were raised on the battlefield of 642. The stone hammer is highly finished and polished. The form of the spear-head agrees with some of the examples figured by Mr. Thomas Wright and Mr. L. Jewitt, as pertaining to the earlier Anglo-Saxon period. It presents a kind of transition from between the shorter Roman bronze and the more elongated iron of the later Anglo-Saxon time. The "feathery pattern" scored on the pottery resembles the rude "herring-bone," or zigzag ornamentation of late Roman and early Anglo-Saxon masonry.

Another and much larger *tumulus* until recently was situated opposite to the parish church at Warrington, and contiguous to the ancient Latchford, by which the British trackway and the great Roman road crossed the Mersey. For some miles both on the east and west, in early times, no other route was practicable; the mosses on the one hand and the tidal estuary on the other presenting insuperable obstacles, especially to heavy traffic. The *tumulus* at Warrington, named the "Mote Hill," was entirely removed in 1852. Pennant had conjectured it to be Roman; Ormerod, Norman; and John Whitaker, Saxon. In a paper read before the Lancashire and Cheshire Historic Society, on November, 1852, Dr. Kendrick gave a detailed account of the excavation, and exhibited the discovered remains. Some of the pottery was rude (apparently Romano-British), and cremated human remains were present, as well as an immense quantity of the remains of animals. Referring to Whitaker's conjecture of the Saxon origin of the mound, or of that race having utilised it, Dr. Kendrick says—

To this opinion I think all the appearances detailed this evening afford strong support.

Mr. Sibson, likewise, who was present at the examination of the hill in 1832, and again in 1841, coincides in this view, and suggests that it originally constituted a *tumulus*, or burial place, raised after the battle fought at Winwick. Dr. Kendrick thought that as the church was dedicated to St. Elphin, slain in 679, the mound might have covered his remains; but the Pagan character of the interment or interments negatives this view.

Mr. W. T. Watkin, in a note to the present writer, says—

Dr. Kendrick's account compared with that of Mr. Sibson evidently shows that the mound was originally a Roman boundary mark, used afterwards in Saxon and medieval times for various purposes. The second excavation merely shows the contents of the mound as they *were thrown in* after the first exploration, with the exception of the well and one or two smaller details. . . . All these things are in accordance with the rules of the Roman *agrimensores*.

This view seems very probable.[10]

---

10. Siculus Flaccus says that it was the practice of some *agrimensores* to place under *termini* ashes, or charcoal, or pieces of broken glass or pottery, or *asses*, or lime, or plaster (gypsum). . . . The writer of a later treatise, or rather compilation, attributed to Boëthius, speaking upon the same subject, enumerates as the objects to be so placed, ashes, or charcoals, or potsherds, or bones, or glass, or *assæ* of iron, or brass, or lime, or plaster, or a fictile vessel.—*The Romans of Britain*, by H. C. Coote F.S.A.

I am inclined to regard these *tumuli*, in the main, as monuments of the site of some great battle or battles, and that amongst others, Maserfeld may be, perhaps, the latest and most important fought in the neighbourhood previous to the disuse of cremation and the general adoption of the modern Christian mode of interment. The whole of these large barrows were evidently erected by people who burned and buried their dead on the spot where the memorial mound or monument was afterwards erected. We know from the Venerable Bede's record, how the body of King Oswald was disposed of. Besides the king being a pious Christian, such a mode of sepulture would not have been adopted by his followers. Penda, on the contrary, was a Pagan, and strongly attached to the superstitions and customs of his Teutonic ancestors. We know that the Pagan Anglo-Saxons in England practised both modes of interment, the burial of the body entire and cremation. Mr. Thomas Wright says—(*Celt, Roman, and Saxon*)

> The custom in this respect appears to have varied with the different tribes who came into the island. In the Anglo-Saxon cemeteries in Kent, cremation is the rare exception to the general rule; while it seems to have been the *predominating practice* among the Angles from Norfolk into the centre of Mercia.

It is, therefore, highly probable, if the battle of Maserfeld was fought in this district, that these tumuli, or some portion of them, were raised by the Pagan Mercian victors over the bodies of chieftains of their party slain in the battle. Nennius says that in the conflict Penda's brother Eawa was slain, and, consequently, he and the other Pagan chieftains who fell in the battle would be interred in Pagan fashion by the victorious survivors.

The oldest Anglo-Saxon poem extant, "Beowulf," the scene of the events of which Mr. D. Haigh, in his *Conquest of Britain by the Saxons*, contends to be the neighbourhood of Hartlepool, in Durham,[11] has preserved to us a description of such a ceremonial in detail. On Beowulf's death, his warriors raised a funeral pile to burn the body. It was—

> *hung round with helmets,*
> *with boards of war, [shields]*
> *and with bright byrnies, [coats of mail]*
> *as he had requested.*

11. This, of course, is disputed by other authorities. Mr. Thorpe regards the only copy now extant as an Anglo-Saxon version of an older Scandinavian poem.

Then the heroes, weeping,
laid down in the midst
the famous chieftain,
their dear lord.
Then began on the hill,
the warriors to awake
the mightiest of funeral fires;
the wood-smoke rose aloft
dark from the fire;
noisily it went,
mingled with weeping.

His faithful followers afterwards erected the barrow over his ashes:—

a mound over the sea;
it was high and broad,
by the sailors over the waves
the beacon of the war-renowned.
They surrounded it with a wall
in the most honourable manner
that wise men
could desire.
They put into the mound
rings and bright gems,
all such ornaments
as before from the hoard
the fierce-minded men
had taken.

The date of the erection of the first parish church at Winwick is not known with certainty. Some contend that it was coeval with the introduction of Christianity into the North of England by Paulinus. Although this is incapable of absolute verification, it is generally conceded that a church must have existed for some time antecedent to the Norman conquest. The Domesday Survey, under the head of "Newton Hundred," seems to confirm this. It says:

Under the reign of King Edward (the Confessor) there were five hides in Newton: one of these was held in demesne. The church of this manor had one carucate of land, and St. Oswald, of this village, had two carucates, *exempt from all taxation.*

74

Mr. Baines says—

In 1828, while digging a vault in the chancel of this church, there were found, at the depth of eight or ten feet below the floor, three human skeletons of gigantic size, laid upon each other, and over them a rude heap of cubical sandstone blocks of irregular dimensions, varying from one to two feet. No remains of coffins were found in the grave, and the history of the occupants of this mysterious tomb remains undiscovered.

It seems, however, not improbable that these interments took place anterior to the building of the church, that the skeletons were the remains of chieftains who perished with Oswald, and that the sacred edifice, dedicated to the warrior saint, was afterwards erected on the spot.

The first known record of the old church at Oswestry is thus referred to by the Rev. D. R. Thomas (His: Diocese of St. Asaph):—

The Parish Church of St. Oswald is first definitely mentioned in 1086 in the Grant of Warin, Vicecomes . . . to the abbot and monks of Shrewsbury Abbey, *dedit eis Ecclesiam Sancti Oswaldi cum decima ville.*

But there is a belief that there was a still earlier one elsewhere than on the present site, which may be due partly to the fact that the town was originally built on some other site, partly to the circumstance that several of the earlier mission stations are still indicated by such names as Maen Tysilio, Croes-Wylan, Cae Croes, and Croes Oswaldt, or The Cross; and to the tradition which Leyland records, "that at Llanforda was a church now" (sixteenth century) "decaid. Sum say this was the paroche church of Oswestre."

I have previously referred to the ancient well, situated about half-a-mile from Winwick Church, known from time immemorial as "St. Oswald's Well." Mr. Edward Baines regards this sacred spring as having been originally formed by the excavation of earth on the spot where Oswald fell, and he fortifies his position by reference to Bede, who says—

Whereupon many took up of the very dust of the place where his body fell, and putting it into water, did much good with it to their friends who were sick. This custom came so much into use, that the earth being carried away by degrees, there remained a hole as deep as the height of a man.

Perhaps the most important objection to the Oswestry site lies in the fact that there is no satisfactory representative of the name of Maserfeld to be found in its neighbourhood.[12] One writer says—

In the vicinity of the town, at a place called by the Welsh '*Cae Naef*' (Heaven's Field) there is a remarkably fine spring of water, which bears the name of Oswald's Well, and over which, as recently as the year 1770, were the ruins of a very ancient chapel likewise dedicated to him.

Commenting on this, Mr. E. Baines says—

The well in that country is a spring and not a fosse, as described by Bede, and is as the well at Winwick.

And he regards this feature as additional evidence in favour of the presumed Lancashire site of the battle. The saint's *well* is not, however, of much value, as Bede makes no mention of any spring, natural or otherwise, and wells dedicated to saints in the "olden time," are common all over the country. Indeed, there is a natural spring near the main highway about a mile to the north of Winwick Church, which is likewise called St. Oswald's well. From Bede's context it is evident Oswald died on the ordinary dry earth, which, in consequence, thenceforth produced greener grass than the surrounding land, and the *soil* was afterwards mixed with water and used medicinally. In England there are at least five different places named after St. Oswald, and, in

12. Mr. Askew Roberts, in his *Contributions to Oswestry History*, has the following:— "Is not all the alluvial tract of country which lies between Buttington and Oswestry, called in the Welsh tongue '*Ystrad Marchell*.' = Strata Marcella, at one end of which stood the once famous monastery of Ystrad Marchell or Strata Marcella? Is it not more likely that Oswald should have been overwhelmed by a combined force of Mercians, Welsh, and Angles somewhere in the large plain of *Ystradmarchell*, which lies on the boundary of the Welsh and Mercian territories, than at Winwick, in Lancashire, and does not the above line prove that 'Oswald from Marchelldy (Marcelde the House or Monastery of Marchell) did to Heaven remove.'—Bonion, writing in *Bygones*, August 6, 1873." This would have more value had the inscription been on Oswestry Church. It is not very probable the Cleric of Winwick would be a Welsh scholar, or that he would translate the Welsh word into Latin in preference to the English one by which the locality was well known. What business had Oswald "somewhere in the large plain of *Ystradmarchell*, which lies on the boundary of the Welsh and Mercian territory," if Penda were the aggressor, as Geoffrey and others testify. Besides, as Mr. Green's maps show, the district in question was, in the seventh century, a long way from either the Mercian or Northumbrian boundary. To be in the locality at all would constitute Oswald the attacking and not the defending party, as Bede's expression, "*pro patria dimicans*," seems to imply.

addition, many ecclesiastical edifices have been dedicated to him.

There is something mysterious, or at least curiously coincident, about this Welsh "*Cae Naef*," or "Heaven's Field," as this latter, according to Bede, is the name of the site of the previous battle in 635, when Oswald defeated and slew Cadwalla. The same authority likewise refers to it as being fought "at a place called Denises-burn, that is Denis's-brook." Dr. Giles says "Dilston is identified with the ancient Deniseburn, but on no authority." Dilston is situated about two miles from Hexham. Sharon-Turner says—

> Camden places this battle at Dilston, formerly Devilston, on a small brook which empties into the Tyne. . . . Smith, with greater probability, makes Errinburn as the rivulet on which Cadwallon perished, and the fields either of Cockley, Hallington, or Bingfield, as the scene of the conflict. The Angles called it Hefenfield, which name, according to tradition, Bingfield bore.

Dr. Smith says that Hallington was anciently Heavenfelth, but adds that probably the whole country from Hallington southward to the Roman wall was originally included in the name. On the place where Oswald is said to have raised a cross, as his standard during the battle, a church was afterwards erected. Thus it would at first sight appear that Oswestry might enter into competition with Bingfield for the site of the Heavenfield struggle, rather than with Winwick for that of Maserfeld. There is, however, one important fact which fatally militates against this. Bede says, referring to the Heavenfield where Cadwalla met his death:

> The place is near the wall with which the Romans formerly enclosed the island from sea to sea, to restrain the fury of the barbarous nations, as has been said before.

The greater probability is as the two engagements are intertwined by the Welsh Bruts, and in the Oswestry and Geoffrey traditions, that the place owes its designation directly to neither the one nor the other; but that, like the sites I have mentioned, the dedication of a church to the saint has been sufficient to confer his name on the locality. That a neighbouring well, under such circumstances, should receive a similar designation, is too ordinary a matter to require special consideration.

It is not at all improbable that, as Geoffrey and the Welsh Bruts both refer to the battle in which Oswald fell as fought at or near Burne, the Oswestry traditions may have originally only had reference to the Battle of Denis-Burn or Denis-brook, in which the Welsh Christian hero, Cadwalla, was slain by his hated rival, the Anglican Christian king Oswald, of Northumbria. It is utterly improbable that the Welsh Christians would dedicate a church to St. Oswald. The first Christian king of Northumbria, Edwin, the friend of Paulinus and Augustine, was slain by Cadwalla, "king of the Britons," or Brit-Welsh, in a battle at Heathfield (Hadfield, in the West Riding of Yorkshire), *A.D.* 633, in which he was aided by the pagan Penda.

The Brit-Welsh Christians and the disciples of Augustine and Paulinus hated each other with more than ordinary sacerdotal intensity, and the former often entered into alliances with the pagan Anglo-Saxons, in order to avenge themselves on their detested rivals. One of the subjects of fierce contention between them, as is well known, related to the time for the celebration of Easter. Bede, referring to the defeat of Edwin at Heathfield and the consequences attendant thereon, says—

> A great slaughter was made in the church or nation of the Northumbrians; and the more so because one of the commanders by whom it was made was a pagan, and the other a barbarian more cruel than a pagan; for Penda, with all the nation of the Mercians, was an idolator and a stranger to the name of Christ; but Cadwalla, although he bore the name and professed himself a Christian, was so barbarous in his disposition and behaviour, that he neither spared the female sex, nor the innocent age of children, but with savage cruelty put them to tormenting deaths, ravaging all their country for a long time, and resolving to cut off all the race of the English within the borders of Britain. Nor did he pay any respect to the *Christian religion which had newly taken root among them*; it being to this day (the 8th century) the custom of Britons not to pay any respect to the faith and religion of the English, nor to correspond with them any more than with pagans.

Unquestionably no Christian church was dedicated to St. Oswald at Oswestry until after the final subjection of the district by the Anglican Christians. The probability therefore is that the locality was merely named, as in the other instances referred to, from the fact that it had become the location of a place of worship dedicated to him, and that gradually the various traditions about the saint and his rivals became inextricably confused. The last syllable "*tre*" is indicative of British influence in the formation of the word Oswestry, as in Pentre, Gladestry, Coventry (in Radnorshire), Tremadoc, Trewilan, Tredegar, etc., which simply means, according to *Spurrell's Welsh Dictionary*, "resort, homestead, home, hamlet, town (used chiefly in composition)." Indeed, Oswestry is more suggestive of Oswy's-tre, and may refer to a successor who, sometime after Oswald's death, built a church and dedicated it to the saintly monarch.

The pagan Mercian king, Penda, was himself slain in the following year by Oswy, the successor to St. Oswald. Bede says:

> The battle was fought near the River Vinwed, which then with the great rains had not only filled its channel, but overflowed its banks, so that many more were drowned in the flight than destroyed by the sword.

Most authorities place this battle at Winwidfield, near Leeds. Mr. Thos. Baines, however (*Historical Notes on the Valley of the Mersey*, His. Soc. Lan. and Ches. Pro. session 5), claims for Winwick the scene of both engagements. He says—

> Penda and upwards of thirty of his principal officers were drowned in their flight, having been driven into the River Winweyde, the waters of which were at that time much swollen by heavy rains. There is no stream in England which is more liable to be suddenly flooded than the stream which joins the Mersey below Winwick[13], and there both the resemblance of the names, and the probability of the fact, induce me to think that Penda met with his death within two or three miles of the place at which Oswald had fallen.

This seems, at first sight, plausible enough, but as Bede distinctly states that "King Oswy concluded the aforesaid war in the country of Loides" (Leeds), Winwidfield must unquestionably have preference over the Lancashire site, as the scene of Penda's discomfiture and death.

It is generally accepted that Oswald died either at Oswestry or Winwick. There are some, however, who accept neither, but contend that the true site of the battle may yet, possibly, be found in a different locality. This appears to be the opinion of Mr. John R. Green. In

---

13. This is a very daring assertion, and is by no means confirmed by a visit to the locality.

support of this view he says (*Making of England*)—

> Though the conversion of Wessex had prisoned it (Mercia) within the central districts of England, heathendom fought desperately for life. Penda remained its rallying point; and the long reign of the Mercian king was in fact one continuous battle with the Cross. But so far as we can judge from his acts, Penda seemed to have looked on the strife of religion in a purely political light. The point of conflict, as before, (that is when Edwin was defeated and slain at Hatfield) seems to have been the dominion over East Anglia. Its possession was vital to Mid-Britain as it was to Northumbria, which needed it to link itself with its West-Saxon subjects in the south; and Oswald must have felt that he was challenging his rival to a decisive combat when he marched, in 642, to deliver the East Anglians from Penda. But his doom was that of Eadwine; for he was overthrown and slain in a battle called the Battle of Maserfeld.

If this view be accepted, the claim of Oswestry must be at once dismissed, while that of Winwick is rendered still more doubtful. But Mr. Green does not state on what authority he relies when he states that Oswald "marched in 642, to deliver the East-Anglians from Penda." In consequence I am unable to test its value or probability. He certainly would not march by either Oswestry or Winwick if such were his destination. This statement, however, appears to be not exactly in accordance with another by Mr. Green, previously quoted, in which he says, referring to the antecedents of the war under Oswy, which followed Oswald's death, and in which Penda was slain near the River Winwid—

> That Oswiu strove to avert the conflict we see from the delivery of his youngest son Ecgfrith as a hostage into Penda's hands. The sacrifice, however, proved useless. *Penda was again the assailant*, and his attack was as vigorous as of old.

If Penda was the assailant, his assault must, in the first instance, have been not on Oswald himself, but on his East-Anglian allies, or Oswald would not have thought of marching in that direction for their relief. But if Penda, having previously humbled the East-Anglians, had become aware of such intention on the part of the Northumbrian monarch, there is nothing improbable in a vigorous warrior of Penda's stamp, by a rapid march, surprising him on the frontier of his own dominions, defeating him, and thus warding off the threatened blow. Under such circumstances Winwick might very probably have been the scene of the conflict. The advocates of Oswestry do not deny the great probability that Oswald had a favourite residence in the locality.

The neighbourhood of Winwick, however, is the undisputed site of a battle in more recent times. After the Duke of Hamilton's defeat at Preston, by Cromwell, in 1648, the former made a stand against his pursuers at a place called "Red Bank," where he was totally routed by the less numerous but highly disciplined army of his more skilful antagonist.

A rude piece of sculpture built in the outer wall, evidently a relic from an older edifice, was long supposed to be a representation of the crest of St. Oswald; but this is disputed by Mr. Edward Baines. He says—

> The heralds assign to that monarch azure, a cross between four lions rampant, or superstition sees in the chained hog the resemblance of a monster in former ages, which prowled over the neighbourhood, inflicting injury on man and beast, and which could only be restrained by the subduing force of the sacred edifice.

This sculpture he regards as not improbably a rude attempt to "represent the crest of the Gerrards—a lion rampant, armed and langued, with a coronet upon the head." This is certainly more probable than the heralds' assignment of "azure, a cross between four lions rampant, or," to Oswald, which is suggestive of medieval Norman-French associations and nomenclature, without the slightest Anglo-Saxon ingredient. The late Mr. T. T. Wilkinson refers to a tradition which asserts that "the demon-pig not only determined the site of St. Oswald's Church, at Winwick, but gave a name to the parish." This attempt to solve the enigma by the assistance of the squeak of a sucking pig, has evidently originated in some rural jesting or lame attempt to divine the connection of the animal with the church and neighbourhood.

This traditionary "monster in former ages, which prowled over the neighbourhood, inflicting injury on man and beast," is worthy of a little more serious attention than has hitherto been paid to it. The legend is evidently but a northern form of the wide-spread Aryan myth concerning Vritra, the dragon, or storm-fiend, who stole the light rain clouds (the "herds of Indra," the Sanscrit "god of the clear heaven, and of light, warmth, and fertilising rain"), and hid them in the cave of the Panis (the dark storm-cloud). Indra, launching his lightning-spear into the black thunder-cloud, (personified by the dragon, snake, or monster whose poisonous breath parched the earth and destroyed the harvest), released the confined waters and thus refertilised the land. The Rev. Sir G. W. Cox, in his *Manual of Mythology*, says—

> In the Indian tales Indra kills the dragon Vritra, and in the old Norse legend Sigurd kills the great snake Fafnir.

The myth survives in the exploits of the patron saint of England, St. George, the slayer of the dragon. In one Teutonic form Odin, or Wodin, hunted the wild boar, the representative of the stormy wind-clouds. His tusk was a type of the lightning. This mythical devouring monster is reproduced in Grendel, the "great scather," in the old Anglo-Saxon poem *Beowulf*, the scene of which Mr. D. Haigh, in his *Conquest of the Britons by the Saxons*, regards as the neighbourhood of Hartlepool, in Durham.

There exists a great diversity of opinion as to the genesis and original habitat of the poem, *Beowulf*. Mr. Frederick Metcalfe, in his *Englishman and Scandinavian*, says—

> There is, however, one Saxon work which tells us of the northern mythology, *Beowulf*, the oldest heroic, or, as some will have it, mythic—perhaps it will be best to call it mytho-heroic—poem in any German language, and which has been pronounced to be older than Homer.

> The date of its composition has been much debated. By Conybeare it was thought, in its present shape, to be the work of the bards about Canute's court. The leading incidents of the plot are as follows:—Beowulf, the son of Ecgtheow and prince in Scania (South Sweden), hearing how for twelve years King Hrothgar and his people in North Jutland had been mightily oppressed by a monster, Grendel, resolves to deliver him, and arrives at Hart Hall, the Jutish palace, as an avenger.

Mr. Benjamin Thorpe, in the preface to his edition of the poem (1855) says—

> With respect to this the oldest heroic poem in any Germanic tongue, my opinion is, that it is not an original production of the Anglo-Saxon muse, but a metrical paraphrase of an heroic Saga composed in the south-west of Sweden, in the old common language of the north, and probably brought to this

country during the sway of the Danish dynasty. It is in this light only that I can view a work evincing a knowledge of northern localities and persons, hardly to be acquired by a native of England in those days of ignorance with regard to remote foreign parts. And what interest could an Anglo-Saxon feel in the valorous feats of his deadly foes, the northmen? in the encounter of a Sweo-Gothic hero with a monster in Denmark? or with a fire-drake in his own country? The answer, I think, is obvious— *none whatever.*

In a note Mr. Thorpe says—

Let us cherish the hope that the original Saga may one day be discovered in some Swedish library.

The only MS. of the poem extant, (MS. *Cott. Vitellius* A. 15), he says—"I take to be of the first half of the eleventh century."

With respect to the strictly historical character of this poem, Mr. Thorpe says—

Preceding editors have regarded the poem of *Beowulf* as a myth, and its heroes as beings of a divine order.[14] To my dull perception these appear as real kings and chieftains of the North, some of them as Hygelac and Offa, entering within the pale of authentic history, while the names of others may have perished, either because the records in which they were chronicled are no longer extant, or the individuals themselves were not of sufficient importance to occupy a place in them.

---

14. Were there no other record of the existence of our own Richard I. than the *Romaunt* bearing his name, and composed within a century of his death, he would unquestionably have been numbered by the Mythists among their shadowy heroes; for among the superhuman feats performed by that pious crusader, we read, in the above mentioned authority, that having torn out the heart of a lion, he pressed out the blood, dipt it in salt, and ate it without bread; that being sick, and longing after pork (which in a land of Moslems and Jews was not to be had),
They took a Sarezyne young and fat And soden full hastely, With powder and with spysory, And with saffron of good colour.
Of this Apician dish 'the kyng eet the flesh and gnew the bones.' Richard afterwards feasts his infidel prisoners on a Saracen's head each, every head having the name of its late owner attached to it on a slip of parchment. Surely all this is as mythic as it is possible to be, and yet Richard is a really historic earth-born personage." Yes, there was a truly historical Richard, as there doubtless was an Arthur, but the Richard and Arthur of romance, nevertheless, are not historical characters, in the strict sense of the word, and ought not to be confounded with them.

Mr. Haigh likewise contends for the historic value of the poem; but attributes its locality to Britain. Some of the legends and traditions of the North of England certainly suggest that the Scandinavian population settled there were either acquainted with the poem or the legendary elements which strongly characterise it, and upon which it is evidently mainly constructed, whatever strictly historical matter, as in the romances of Richard Cœur de Lion, Charlemagne, Arthur, and others, may have become incorporated therewith. (See note following).

Note:—At the meeting of the British Association, held at York, in 1861, Dr. Phene, F.S.A., &c., read a paper on Scandinavian and Pictish customs on the Anglo-Scottish Border. He spoke of the persistent retention of curious customs, and the handing down from generation to generation of the traditionary lore of ages long past, and then referred to some of those which were corroborated by ancient monuments of an unusual kind still famous on the Scottish border. These consisted of sculptured stones, earth works, and actual ceremonies. Quoting from former writers, from family pedigrees, and other documents, he showed that the estates to which this traditionary lore pertained, had been held alternately by those claiming under the respective nationalities, or more local powers, and which from their natural defensive features must have been places of border importance earlier than history records.

The district was occupied by the descendants—often still traceable—of Danes, Jutes, Frisians, Picts, Scots, Angles, and Normans; and by a comparison of several of the languages of these people, as well ancient as now existing, and also of the Gothic, it was shown in relation to a particular class of the most curious monuments, that the Norse "*ormr,*" Anglo-Saxon "*vyrm,*" old German "*wurm,*" Gothic "*vaúrms,*" pronounced like our word worm; and the word "*lint,*" or "*lind,*" also German, and the Norse "*linni,*" are all equivalent, and mean serpent; and in some cases the two words are united as in modern German "*lindwurm,*" and the Danish and Swedish "*lindorm.*"

On this apparently rested the names of some of the places having these strange traditions, as Linton or serpent town, Wormiston or worm's (ormr's) town, Lindisfarne, the Farne serpent island, now Holy Island, &c., and also the various worm hills, or serpent mounds of those localities. It was curious that the contests to which the traditions referred (like that of St. George) were sometimes with two dragons, as shown on a sculptured stone in Linton Church, and on a similar stone at Lyngby, in Denmark, in the churchyard, where there was a tradition that two dragons had their haunt near the church.

From these and other facts, the author concluded that the contests were international, and in the case of two dragons, an allied foe, either national, religious, or both, was overcome. He showed from the Scottish seals that Scotland used the dragon as an emblem, apparently deriving it from the Picts; that the Scandinavians also used it, and that these nationalities were antagonistic to the Saxon. In the time of David the First of Scotland, the first great centralisation of Saxon power took place, and the powerful family of the Cumyns took, apparently by conquest, at least two of the localities having these strange traditions.

And as the political object was to suppress the Celtic and Scandinavian, or other local national feeling, there could be little doubt that however they obtained them, the persons dispossessed were of one or other of the Northern tribes. Hence probably the middle-age tradition of the slaying of the serpent or dragon, or the serpent or dragon bearer, on the Anglo-Scottish border. But he considered such traditions would hardly have originated through such conquests, had not previous marvellous stories existed of the prowess and conquest by the dragon (bearers) of the lands they invaded, all the wonders of which would be transferred to the conqueror's conqueror. Hence these stories were not to be set aside with a sneer, as in them was a germ of history, giving us, perhaps, the only insight we could obtain of the prehistoric customs and mythology of some of the ancient tribes of Britain.

Earthen mounds, *tumuli*, standing stones, &c., still existed in some of these localities, with all of which the dragon serpent or worm was associated in the legends. The author described his personal experiences in the still existing dragon ceremonies in the south of France and Spain, which were always either on the present national or former less important provincial frontiers, and which still formed the subjects of great ecclesiastical ceremonies. One of the high ecclesiastical dignitaries of the north of England—the Bishop of Durham—is in the position of having to take part in such a ceremony.

Whenever a bishop of that diocese enters the manor of Sockburn for the first time, the Lord of the Manor, who holds under the see of Durham, subject to the following tenure, has to present the Bishop, "*in the middle of the river Tees*, if the river is fordable, with the falchion wherewith the champion Conyers destroyed the *worm, dragon*, or *fiery flying serpent* which destroyed man, woman, and child" in that district, and an ancient altar called "*Greystone*" still marks where the dragon was buried.—*Manchester Examiner*.

Mr. John R. Green (*The Making of England*) says:

The song as we have it now is a poem of the eighth century, the work it may be of some English missionary of the days of Beda and Boniface, who gathered in the homeland of his race the legend of its earlier prime.

After referring to the interpolations in which there "is a distinctly Christian element, contrasting strongly with the general heathen current of the whole," Mr. Sweet, in his *Sketch of the History of the Anglo-Saxon Poetry*, in Hazlitt's edition of Warton's *His. of English Poetry*, says—

Without these additions and alterations it is certain that we have in *Beowulf* a poem composed before the Teutonic conquest of Britain. The localities are purely continental; the scenery is laid amongst the Goths of Sweden and the Danes; in the episodes the Swedes, Frisians, and other continental tribes appear, while there is no mention of England, or the adjoining countries and nations.

Mr. Jno. Fenton, in an able article on "Easter" in the *Antiquary* for April, 1882, says—

To us in western lands the equinox is the beginning of spring and the new life of the year; but in the east it is the beginning of summer, when the early harvest is also ripe, when the sun is parching the grass and drying up the wells, when, as Egyptian folk-lore has it, a serpent wanders over the earth, infecting the atmosphere with its poisonous breath.[15]

These mythical huge worms, serpents, dragons, wild boars, and

15. *Klunzinger: Upper Egypt, 184.*

other monsters, "harvest blasters," are still very common in the North of England. The famous "Lambton worm," of huge dimensions and poisonous breath, when coiled round a hill, was pacified with copious draughts of milk, and his blood flowed freely when he was pierced by the spear-heads attached to the armour of the returned Crusader. The Linton worm curled itself round a hill, and by its poisonous breath destroyed the neighbouring animal and vegetable life. The Pollard worm is described as "a venomous serpent which did much harm to man and beast," while that at Stockburn is designated as the "worm, dragon, or fiery flying serpent, which destroyed man, woman, and child."

In the ancient romance in English verse, which celebrates the deeds of the renowned Sir Guy, of Warwick, is the following quaint description of a Northumberland dragon, slain by the hero:—

A messenger came to the king.
Syr king he sayd, lysten me now,
For bad tydinges I bring you.
In Northumberlande there is no man,
But that they be slayne everychone;
For there dare no man route,
By twenty myle rounde aboute,
For doubt of a fowle dragon,
That sleath men and beastes downe.
He is blacke as any cole,
Ragged as a rough fole;
His body from the navill upwards.
No man may it pierce it is so harde;
His neck is great as any summere;
He renneth as swift as any distrere;
Pawes he hath as a lyon;
All that he toucheth he sleath dead downe,
Great winges he hath to flight,
That is no man that bare him might,
There may no man fight him agayne,
But that he sleath him certayne;
For a fowler beast then is he,
Ywis of none never heard ye.

The said Guy, amongst other marvellous exploits, killed at "Winsor,"

A bore of passing might and strength,
Whose like in England never was,

For hugenesse both in breadth and length.

Mr. Barrett, a saddler, of Manchester, with antiquarian taste, in an illuminated MS., now in the Chetham Library, refers to an old tradition concerning a dragon whose den was amongst the red sandstone rocks in the neighbourhood of Lymm, about five miles from Warrington. Geoffrey of Monmouth, in Merlin's prophesy especially, often refers to these mythical monsters; and the *Anglo-Saxon Chronicle* is equally expressive in attributing disaster to their influences. In the latter work we read:

> *A.D.* 793. This year dire forewarnings came over the land of the Northumbrians, and miserably terrified the people; these were excessive whirlwinds and lightnings; and fiery dragons were seen flying in the air. A great famine soon followed these tokens.

Mr. Baring-Gould says, as recently as the year 1600,—

> A German writer would illustrate a thunderstorm destroying a crop of corn by a picture of a dragon devouring the produce of the field with his flaming tongue and iron teeth.

That this tradition at Winwick respecting a "monster in former ages, which prowled over the neighbourhood, inflicting injury on man and beast," is a legitimate descendant from our Aryan ancestors' personification of natural phenomena, seems very apparent, and aptly illustrates what Sir G. W. Dasent terms the "toughness of tradition," especially when interwoven with the marvellous or supernatural. Mr. Walter K. Kelly, in his *Curiosities of Indo-European Tradition and Folk-Lore,* says—

> These phenomena were noted and designated with a watchfulness and a wealth of imagery which made them the principal groundwork of all the Indo-European mythologies and superstitions. The thunder was the bellowing of a mighty beast or the rolling of a wagon. The lightning was a sinuous serpent, or a spear shot straight athwart the sky, or a fish darting in zigzags through the waters of heaven. The stormy winds were howling dogs or wolves; the ravages of the whirlwind that tore up the earth *were the work of a wild boar.*[16]

---

16. There exists yet a traditionary superstition very prevalent in Lancashire and its neighbourhood to the effect that pigs can '*see the wind.*' I accidentally heard the observation made, not long ago, in the city of Manchester, in what is termed 'respectable society,' and no one present audibly dissented. (Continued next page).

Mr. Fiske, in his *Myths and Myth-makers*, says that these mythical monsters:

> . . . . .not only steal the daylight, but they parch the earth and wither the fruits, and they slay vegetation during the winter months.

These traditionary "Harvest Blasters," as they are sometimes styled, have a wide range, and are not confined even to the various branches of the Aryan race.

Most writers agree in assigning the origin of heraldry, in the modern acceptation of the term, to the crusades. At least little is recorded concerning the "science," or "art," as it is sometimes termed, previously to the middle of the twelfth century. It was found necessary during the religious wars in the east that the knights should wear some device or distinguishing badge on the field of battle, on account of the diversity of the languages spoken by the combatants, and hence the term "cognizance" was often applied to these symbols. This, in the following century, eventuated in the adoption of the warlike badges or "arms" of the original bearers by their families. They afterwards became hereditary characteristics, and hence the development of the *quasi* science. These devices were figured on crest, banner, and shield. One authority (*Pen. Cyclop.*) says—

> The crest is said to have been carved on light wood, or made of leather, *in the shape of some animal, real or fictitious*, and fastened by a fillet of silk round the helmet, over which was a large piece of fringed samit or taffeta, pointed with a tassel at the end.

> The custom of conferring crests as distinguishing marks seems to have originated with Edward III., who, in 1333 (*Rot. Pat.*, 9 Edward III.), granted one to William Montacute, Earl of Salisbury, his 'tymbre,' as it is called, of the eagle. By a further grant, in the thirteenth of the same king (*Rot. Vasc.*, 13 Edward III., m. 4), the grant of this crest was made hereditary, and the manor of Wodeton given in addition to support its dignity.

I am inclined, notwithstanding, to regard heraldry in its more extend-

---

One or two individuals, indeed, remarked that they had often heard such was the case, and seemed to regard the phenomenon as related to the strong scent and other instincts peculiar to animals of the chase. Indeed, Dr. Kuhn says that in Westphalia this phase of the superstition is the prevalent one. There pigs are said to smell the wind.—*Traditions, Superstitions, and Folk-Lore, p. 69.*

ed significance, that is if the term can properly be applied to practices anterior to the establishment of heralds, as of much greater antiquity than the crusades. Herodotus tells us that the Carians first set the Greeks the example of fastening crests upon their helmets, and of putting devices upon their shields. The *"totems,"* or beast symbols, of our savage ancestors undoubtedly preceded the medieval practice, and influenced its incipient development. The "White Horse" of Hengist, the "Raven" of the Scandinavian Vikings, the "Golden Dragon" of the kings of Wessex, as well as others, might be mentioned, which clearly demonstrate this position. Uther, the father of Arthur, according to Geoffrey of Monmouth, caused "two dragons to be made of gold, which was done with wondrous nicety of workmanship." The *quasi*-historian adds—

He made a present of one to the cathedral church of Winchester, but reserved the other for himself to be carried along with him to his wars. From this time, therefore, he was called Uther Pendragon, which in the British tongue signifies the dragon's head.

Indeed, amongst savage nations at the present or relatively recent time, we find *"totems"* or symbols, such as beaver, snake, hare, cornstalk, black hawk, dog, wolf, bear, beaver, little bear, crazy horse, and sitting bull, not only used by the warrior chiefs, but even the tribes sometimes take their names therefrom.

Mr. E. B. Tylor, in his *Early History of Mankind*, says—

More than twenty years ago, Sir George Grey called attention to the divisions of the Australians into families, and distinguished by the name of some animal or vegetable, which served as their crest or *kobong*.

The Indian tribes (of America) are usually divided into clans, each distinguished by a *totem* (Algonquin *do-daim*, that is 'town mark,') which is commonly some animal, as a bear, wolf, deer, etc., which may be compared on the one hand to a crest, and on the other to a surname.

Indeed, until very recently, some of our own regiments had their "beast *totem*" in the shape of a goat, a bear, or a tiger, which generally marched at the head of the corps. The goat, I believe, yet survives, and the men of one regiment are designated "tigers" to this day.

The crest is evidently one of the oldest, if not the oldest, forms in which the beast symbol was displayed. The bronze Roman helmet, or rather bust or head of Minerva, found at Ribchester, in 1796, had originally a sphinx as a crest. This appendage, however, having become detached, has since been lost. The gladiators' helmet decorations, in the pictures found at Pompeii, are generally plumes or tufts of horsehair, but some of their shields exhibit devices suggestive of those of more recent date. The Roman historians, recording the events pertaining to the great Cimbri-Teutonic invasion rather more than a century before the Christian era, state that each of the fifteen thousand horsemen, which formed the *élite* of the army of Bojorix, "bore upon his helmet the head of some savage beast, with its mouth gaping wide."

Osman, the son of Ertoghrul, was the founder of the Turkish empire (*A.D.*1288-1326). One writer (*Pen. Cyc.*) says—

The name Osman is of Arabic origin (Othman), and signifies literally the bone-breaker; but it also designates a species of large vulture, usually called the royal vulture, and in this latter acceptation it was given to the son of Ertoghrul.

The Rev. Isaac Taylor, in his *Etruscan Researches*, referring to the origin of the tribal "*totem*" of the Asena horde, afterwards named Turks, says—

It is not difficult to discover the genesis of the legend. It has been already shown that the ancient Ugric word *sena* meant a 'man.' The analogy of a host of ancient tribe-names leaves little doubt that the Asena simply called themselves 'the men.' This obvious etymology of the name having in lapse of time become obscure by linguistic changes, the word *schino*, a wolf, was assumed to be the true source of the national appellation, and the myth came into existence as a means of accounting for the name of the nation which proudly called itself the 'wolf-race,' and bore the wolves' heads as its '*totem.*'

It is said the Kabyls tattoo figures of animals on their foreheads, cheeks, nose, or temples, in order to distinguish their various tribes. A similar practice obtains generally in central Africa and the Caroline archipelago.

The plague, sent by Artemis to punish Æneus, who had neglected to offer up to her a portion of a sacrifice, was a "monstrous boar," afterwards slain by Meleagros, Atalanta, and others, in the famous Kalydonian hunt, is evidently a Greek form of a mythical "monster, which in former ages prowled over the neighbourhood, inflicting injury on man and beast."

The boar, or the boar's head, was a favourite helmet crest or "totem" amongst our Teutonic ancestors, both Scandinavian and German. This animal was sacred to the goddess Friga, or Freya, whom Tacitus, in his "Germania," styles the "mother of the gods," and from whom our Friday is named. She was propitiated by the warriors in order to secure her protection in battle. This practice is often referred to in the sagas, as well as in the earliest known example of Anglo-Saxon poetry extant, *Beowulf.* The following illustrations are from this remarkable poem:—

When we in battle our mail hoods defended,
When troops rushed together and boar-crests crashed.

Then commanded he to bring in
The boar, an ornament to the head,
The helmet lofty in war.

Surrounded with lordly chains,
Even as in days of yore,
The weapon-smith had wrought it,
Had wondrously finished it,
Had set it round with shapes of swine,
That never afterwards brand or war-knife
Might have power to bite it.
They seemed a boar's form
To bear over their cheeks;
Twisted with gold,
Variegated and hardened in the fire;
This kept the guard of life.

At the pile was
Easy to be seen
The mail shirt covered with gore,
The hog of gold,
The boar hard as iron.

In the episode relating the events attendant on the battle of Finsburgh, in the same poem, we find similar importance attached to the boar, as the warrior's protector. We read—

Of the martial Scyldings,
The best of warriors,

On the pile was ready;
At the heap was
Easy to be seen
The blood-stained tunic,
The swine all golden,
The boar iron-hard, etc.

In the *Life of Merlin*, Arthur and his kinsman, Hoel, are described as "two lions," and "two moons." In the same poem, Hoel is styled the "Armorican boar."

In the Welsh poem, *The Gododin*, by Aneurin, are several allusions to the boar and the bull, as warlike appellations:—

It was like the tearing onset of the woodland boar;
Bull of the army in the mangling fight.

The furze was kindled by the ardent spirit, the bull of conflict.

And those shields were shivered before the herd of the roaring Beli. [17]

The boar proposed a compact in front of the course—the great plotter.

Adan, the son of Ervai, there did pierce,
Adan pierced the haughty boar.

Mr. F. Metcalfe, in his *Englishman and Scandinavian*, says—

Indeed this porcine device was common to all the Northern nations who worshipped Freya and Freyr. The helmet of the Norwegian king, Ali, was called Hildigölltr, the boar of war, and was prized beyond measure by his victors (*Prose Edda, I.*, 394).

But long before that Tacitus (*Germ.*, 45) had recorded that the Esthonians, east of the Baltic, wore swine-shaped amulets, as a symbol of the mother of the gods.

Tacitus adds—

This (the wild-boar symbol) serves instead of weapons or any other defence, and gives safety to the servant of the goddess, even in the midst of the foe.

This connection of the boar with the religious ceremonies and warlike exploits of our pagan ancestors is often referred to in the Edda. The valiant Norseman believed that when he entered Walhalla he should join the combats of the warriors each morning, and hack

17. The Rev. Jno. Williams, in a note to his translation of *The Gododin*, says:—"Beli, son of Benlli, a famous warrior in North Wales.

93

and hew away as in earthly conflict, till the slain for the day had been "chosen," and mealtime arrived, when the vanquished and victorious returned together to feast on the "everlasting boar" (*sæhrimnir*), and carouse on mead and ale with the Æsir. The boar's head, which figured so conspicuously in the Christmas festivities of our ancestors, is evidently a relic, like the mistletoe and the yule-log, of pagan times.

There is nothing, therefore, improbable in the proposition that the standard, *totem*, or helmet-crest of some devastating Teutonic chieftain like Penda, the ferocious pagan conqueror of Oswald, may have been of this porcine character. The Christian adherents of the Northumbrian king and saint would very easily confound him and the devastation attendant upon his victorious march through their country, with the dethroned and abhorred pagan deity whose emblem formed his crest or "*totem*," as well as with the older wild boar storm-fiend, or "the monster who prowled over the neighbourhood, inflicting injury on man and beast," and for the subdual of which the sanctity of the edifice of the saintly monarch was alone effectual.

In the prophecy attributed to Merlin, King Arthur is described as the wild boar of Cornwall, that would "devour" his enemies. The mingling of ancient superstitious fears with the more modern Christianity, especially with reference to such matters as charms, prophylactics, etc., is of very common occurrence even at the present day. Sir John Lubbock, in his *Origin of Civilisation and the Primitive Condition of Man*, says—

When man, either by natural progress or the influence of a more advanced race, rises to a conception of a higher religion, he still retains his old beliefs, which linger on side by side with, and yet in utter opposition to, the higher creed. The new and more powerful spirit is an addition to the old pantheon, and diminishes the importance of the older deities; gradually the worship of the latter sinks in the social scale, and becomes confined to the ignorant and young. Thus a belief in witchcraft still flourishes amongst our agricultural labourers and the lowest class in our great cities, and the deities of our ancestors survive in the nursery tales of our children. We must, therefore, expect to find in each race traces—nay, more than traces—of lower religions.

Some parties regard the Winwick sculpture as "St. Anthony's pig," but they acknowledge they know of no connection of that saint with the parish. But, as I have shown in the previous chapter, "the deeds of one mythical hero are sure, when he is forgotten, to be attributed to some other man of mark, who for the time being fills the popular fancy." Keightley, in his *Fairy Mythology*, says—

Every extraordinary appearance is found to have its extraordinary cause assigned, a cause always connected with the *history* or *religion, ancient or modern,* of the country, and not unfrequently *varying with the change of faith.* The mark on Adam's Peak, in Ceylon, is by the Buddhists ascribed to Buddha; by the Mohammedans to Adam.

Mr. Mackenzie Wallace, in his *Russia,* speaking of the Finns and their Russian neighbours, says—

The friendly contact of two such races naturally led to a curious blending of the two religions. The Russians adopted many customs from the Finns, and the Finns adopted still more from the Russians. When Yumala and the other Finnish deities did not do as they were desired, their worshippers naturally applied for protection or assistance to the Madonna and the 'Russian god.' If their own traditional magic rites did not suffice to ward off evil influences, they naturally tried the effect of crossing themselves as the Russians do in moments of danger.

At the harvest festivals, Tchuvash peasants have been known to pray first to their own deities and then to St. Nicholas, the miracle-worker, who is the favourite saint of the Russian peasantry. This dual worship is sometimes recommended by the Yornzi—a class of men who correspond to the medicine men among the Red Indians. . . . .popular imagination always uses heroic names as pegs on which to hang traditions.

Bishop Percy, in the preface to his translation of *Mallet's Northern Antiquities,* says—

Nothing is more contagious than superstition, and therefore we must not wonder if, in ages of ignorance, one wild people catch up from another, though of very different race, the most arbitrary and groundless opinions, or endeavour to imitate them in such rites and practices as they are told will recommend them to the gods, or avert their anger.

Jacob Grimm says (*Deutsche Mythologie*)—

A people whose faith is falling to pieces will save here and there a fragment of it, by fixing it on a new and unpersecuted object of veneration.

It appears, therefore, that the Winwick monster, in this respect, is but an apt illustration of ordinary mythological transference of attributes or emblems, which in no way invalidates the more remote origin to which I have ascribed it, or its connection with the totem or beast symbol of the heathen warrior. The boar, indeed, has been a sacred symbol for ages amongst the Aryan nations. Herodotus (b. 3, c. 59) says that the Eginetæ, after defeating the Samians in a sea-fight, "cut off the prows of their boats, which represented the figure of a boar, and dedicated them in the temple of Minerva, in Egina."

The Rev. Sir G. W. Cox, in his *Introduction to Mythology and Folk-Lore*, referring to the Greek war god Arês, says—

In the Odyssey his name is connected with Aphrodite, whose love he is said to have obtained; but other traditions tell us that when she seemed to favour Adonis, Arês changed himself into a boar, which slew the youth of whom he was jealous.

The Mussulman's abhorrence of roast pork is well known. Amongst the Turkomans of Central Asia (the ancient home of our Aryan ancestors) the prowess of the living animal is likewise regarded with a strange superstitious dread, evidently akin to some more ancient belief in the supernatural attributes of the animal. Arminius Vámbéry, in his *Travels in Central Asia* (having narrowly escaped serious injury from a wild porcine assailant), informs us he was seriously assured by a Turkoman friend that he might regard himself as very lucky, inasmuch as "death by the wound of a wild boar would send even the most pious Mussulman *nedgis* (unclean) into the next world, where a hundred years' burning in purgatorial fire would not purge away his uncleanness."

Since the above was written I have perceived a passage in Mr. Fiske's essay on *Werewolves*, in his *Myths and Myth-makers*, that seems not only to strengthen the conjecture that the boar was the crest or "*totem*" of the pagan Penda, but likewise the probability of the influence of the older mythical story with which I have associated it. The boar, it must be remembered, in all the Indo-European mythologies, is associated with stormy wind and lightning. Mr. Fiske, referring to what he terms one of the "more striking characteristics of primitive thinking," namely, "the close community of nature which it assumes between man and brute," says—

> The doctrine of metempsychosis, which is found in some shape or other all over the world, implies a fundamental identity between the two: the Hindu is taught to respect the flocks browsing in the meadow, and will on no account lift his hand against a cow, for who knows but that it may be his own grandmother? The recent researches of Mr. Lennan and Mr. Herbert Spencer have served to connect this feeling with the primeval worship of ancestors and with the savage customs of *totemism*. . . . This kind of worship still maintains a languid existence as the state religion of China, and it still exists as a portion of Brahmanism; but in the Vedic religion it is to be seen in all its native simplicity. According to the ancient Aryan, the Pitris, or 'Fathers' (*Lat. Patres*) live in the sky along with Yama, the great original Pitri of mankind. . . .
>
> Now if the storm-wind is a host of Pitris, or one great Pitri, who appeared as a fearful giant, and is also a pack of wolves or wish-hounds, or a single savage dog or wolf, the inference is obvious to the mythopœic mind that men may become wolves, at least after death. And to the uncivilised thinker this inference is strengthened, as Mr. Spencer has shown by evidence registered on his own tribal 'totem' or heraldic emblem. The bears and lions and leopards of heraldry are the degenerate descendants of the '*totem*' of savagery which designated a tribe by a beast symbol. To the untutored mind there is everything in a name; and the descendant of Brown Bear, or Yellow Tiger, or Silver *Hyena*, cannot be pronounced unfaithful to his own style of philosophising if he regards *his ancestors, who career about his hut in the darkness of the night,* as belonging to whatever order of beasts his 'totem' associations may suggest.

In the Volsung tale of the Northern mythology the "gods of the bright heaven" had to make atonement to the sons of Reidmar, whose brother they had slain. This brother was named "the otter."

Modern surnames have been derived from very varied sources, including trades, locations, and individual characteristics. Many, identical with birds, beasts, and fishes, may have originally been what are vulgarly termed "nicknames," or they may be corrupt modern renderings of very different ancient words, such as Haddock, from Haydock, a township in Lancashire; Winter, from vintner; and Sumner from summoner, &c. Nevertheless, the old tribal *"totem"* or heraldic device of a feudal superior may have given rise to some of the following: Wolf, Lyon, Hog, Bull, Bullock, Buck, Hart, Fox, Lamb, Hare, Poynter, Badger, Beaver, Griffin, Raven, Hawk, Eagle, Stork, Crane, Woodcock, Gull, Nightingale, Cock, Cockerell, Bantam, Crow, Dove, Pigeon, Lark, Swallow, Martin, Wren, Teal, Finch, Jay, Sparrow, Partridge, Peacock, Goose, Gosling, Bird, Fish, Salmon, Sturgeon, Gudgeon, Herring, Roach, Pike, Sprat, &c.

Some flowers and plants may likewise have formed badges or tribal or family symbols or "quarterings," and thus given rise to surnames. We have several of this class, such as Plantagenet (the broom), Rose, Lily, Primrose, Heath, Broome, Hollyoak, Pine, Thorne, Hawthorne, Hawes, Hyacinth, Crabbe, Crabtree, Crabstick, &c. The leek, the Welshman's "totem," is not an uncommon name, though generally spelled Leak. I never, however, heard of such names as Shamrock or Thistle. On the other hand, many families have reversed the process and adopted a symbol or crest from a real or fancied similarity of their names and those of the selected objects. The figure of a dog is borne on the arms of the Talbot family, whence, perhaps, the name. The talbot is a dog noted for his quick scent and eager pursuit of game.

Jacob Grimm (*Deutsche Mythologie,*) says:—

Even in the middle ages, Landscado (scather of the land) was a name borne by noble families. . . . .Swans, ravens, wolves, stags, bears, and lions, will join the heroes, to render them assistance; and that is how animal figures in the scutcheons and helmet insignia of heroes are in many cases to be accounted for, though they may arise from other causes too, *e.g.*, the ability of certain heroes to transform themselves at will into wolf or swan.

Mr. Charles Elton (*Origins of English History,*) says—

The names of several tribes, or the legends of their origin, show that an animal, or some other real or imaginary object, was chosen as a crest or emblem, and was probably regarded with a superstitious veneration. A powerful family or tribe would feign to be descended from a swan or a water-maiden, or a 'white lady,' who rose from the moon-beams on the lake. The moon herself was claimed as the ancestress of certain families. The legendary heroes are turned into 'swan-knights,' or fly away in the form of wild-geese. The tribe of the 'Ui Duinn,' who claimed St. Bridgit as their kinswoman, wore for their crest the figure of a lizard, which appeared at the foot of the oak-tree above her shrine.

We hear of 'griffins' by the Shannon, of 'calves' in the country around Belfast; the men of Ossory were called by a name which signifies the wild red-deer! There are similar instances from Scotland in such names as 'Clan Chattan,' or the Wild Cats, and in the animal crests which have been borne from the most ancient times as the emblems or cognizances of the chieftains. The early Welsh poems will furnish another set of examples. The tribes who fought at Catraeth are distinguished by the bard as wolves, bears, or ravens; the families which claim descent from Caradock or Oswain take the boar or the raven for their crest. The followers of 'Cian the Dog' are called the 'dogs of war,' and the chieftain's house is described as the stone or castle of 'the white dogs.'

The writer, in the *Pen. Cyclop.*, of the memoir of Owen Glendwr, says—

It was at this juncture that Glendwr revived the ancient prophecy that Henry IV. should fall under the name of 'Moldwary,' or 'the cursed of God's mouth'; and styling himself 'the Dragon,' assumed a badge representing that monster with a star above, in imitation of Uther, whose victories over the Saxons were foretold by the appearance of a star with a dagger threatening beneath. Percy was denoted 'the Lion,' from the crest of his family; and on Sir Edward Mortimer they bestowed the title of 'the Wolf.'

Hugh of Avranche, Earl of Chester, was called Hugh Lupus, from his cognizance or favourite device of a wolf's head.

Shakspere has preserved to us at least two noteworthy instances in which the "*totem*" or beast symbol of our savage ancestors survived, with its original significance, until the period of the "Wars of the Roses." In the Second Part of *King Henry VI.* (Act 5, Scene 1), Warwick exclaims:—

Now, by my father's badge, old Nevil's crest,
The rampant bear chain'd to the ragged staff,
This day I'll wear aloft my burgonet
(As on a mountain top the cedar shows,
That keeps his leaves in spite of any storm),

99

Even to affright thee with the view thereof.

To which boast Clifford replies:—

And from thy burgonet I'll rend thy bear,
And tread it underfoot with all contempt,
Despite the bearward that protects the bear.

Warwick, in the following scene, amidst the carnage of battle, shouts:—

Clifford of Cumberland, 'tis Warwick calls!
And if thou dost not hide thee from the bear,
Now—when the angry trumpet sounds alarm,
And dead men's cries do fill the empty air—
Clifford, I say, come forth and fight with me!

The expression "*dead* men's cries do fill the empty air," I have hitherto regarded, as doubtless most other readers of Shakespeare have done, as either a misprint or an obsolete form of expression, meaning, in the more modern English, "*dying* men's cries do fill the empty air." Taken in connection, however, with the continual reference of Warwick to the "rampant bear" as his ancestral "totem" or beast symbol, I am inclined to think it is not improbable that Shakespeare, who has made use of such an enormous number of other superstitious fancies as poetic images, as well as illustrations of character, may have had in his mind the old belief that the souls of ancestors, "Pitris," or "Fathers," careered and howled amongst the storm-winds in the form indicated by their beast symbol or tribal "*totem.*" Poetically, the thought is singularly appropriate to the storm and strife of the battlefield, and especially to the frenzied agony engendered by the horrors too often attendant upon "*domestic* fury and fierce *civil* strife." Referring to, and quoting from, the *Exodus*, a poem of the Cœdman school, Mr. Green (*The Making of England*) says—

The wolves sang their dread evensong; the fowls of war, greedy of battle, dewy feathered, screamed around the host of Pharaoh, as wolf howled and eagle screamed round the host of Penda.

Shakespeare places in the mouth of *Calphurnia*, when recounting the prodigies which preceded Cæsar's assassination, the following remarkable words:—

The graves have yawn'd and yielded up their dead:

100

Fierce fiery warriors fight upon the clouds
In ranks and squadrons and right form of war,
Which drizzled blood upon the Capitol;
The noise of battle hurtled in the air,
Horses did neigh and dying men did groan,
And ghosts did shriek and squeal about the streets.

When beggars die there are no comets seen:
The heavens themselves blaze forth the death of princes.

Again, in *Richard III.* (Act 3, Scene 2), *Stanley's* messenger informs Hastings that his master had commissioned him to say he had dreamt that night "the boar (Richard) had raised off his helm." This, he adds, his master regards as a warning to Hastings and himself—

To shun the danger that his soul divines.

The boar was the cognizance, crest, or "*totem*" of Richard. In the fourth scene of the same act, Hastings, on hearing his death sentence, exclaims:

Woe! woe for England! not a whit for me;
For I, too fond, might have prevented this:
Stanley did dream the boar did raise his helm;
But I disdain'd it, and did scorn to fly.

In Act 4, Scene 4, Stanley, addressing Sir Christopher Urswick, says:—

Sir Christopher, tell Richmond this from me:
That in the sty of this most bloody boar,
My son, George Stanley, is frank'd up in hold;
If I revolt, off goes young George's head;
The fear of that withholds my present aid.

In Richmond's address to his army, in the second scene of the fifth act, the Aryan personification of the destroying storm-wind and "harvest blaster," as well as "the monster in former ages, which prowled over the neighbourhood, inflicting injury on man and beast," is very distinctly indicated, and adds another link to the chain of evidence by which I have endeavoured to justify the hypothesis that the rude sculpture of Winwick may represent the crest or "totem" of Penda, the ruthless pagan victor in the disastrous fight at Maserfeld, in the year 642. Richmond says:—

The wretched, bloody, and usurping boar,
That spoiled your summer fields and fruitful vines,
Swills your warm blood like wash, and makes his trough
In your embowell'd bosoms—this foul swine
Lies now even in the centre of this isle,
Near to the town of Leicester.

There is an old rhyming couplet, referring to the three personages who were Richard's chief advisers or instruments, in his usurpation, Ratcliffe, Catesby and Lovel, which throws additional light on this beast symbolism:—

The rat and the cat, and Lovel the dog,
Do govern all England under the hog.

Amongst our Scandinavian predecessors the customs and superstitions now under consideration seem to have been deeply rooted. Sir G. W. Dasent, in the introduction to his translation of the Icelandic saga, the *Story of Brunt Njal*, says the Icelander believed in wraiths and patches and guardian spirits, who followed particular persons, and belonged to certain families—

A belief which seems to have sprung from the habit of regarding body and soul as two distinct beings, which at certain times took each a separate bodily shape. Sometimes the guardian spirit or Jylgja took a human shape, and at others its *form took that of some animal to foreshadow the character of the man to whom it belonged.* Thus it becomes a bear, a wolf, an ox, and even a fox, in men. The Jylgja of women were fond of taking the shape of swans. To see one's own Jylgja was unlucky, and often a sign that a man was 'fey,' or death-doomed. So, when Thord Freedman-son tells Njal that he sees the goat wallowing in its gore in the 'town' of Bergthirsknoll, the foresighted man tells him that he has seen his own Jylgja, and that he must be doomed to die. Finer and nobler natures often saw the guardian spirits of others . . . From the Jylgja of the individual it was easy to rise to the still more abstract notion of the guardian spirits of a family, who sometimes, if a great change in the house is about to begin, even show themselves as hurtful to some member of the house. He believed also that some men had more than one shape (*voru eigi einhamir*); that they could either take the shapes of animals, as bears or wolves, and so work mischief; or that without undergoing bodily change, an access of rage and strength came over them, and more especially towards night, which made them more than a match for ordinary men.

To those who may fancy that in this inquiry I have carried conjecture and apparent analogy beyond the domain of legitimate critical inference, I answer in the words of Professor Gervinus, in his comments on the sonnets of Shakespeare—

The caution of the critic does not require that we should repudiate a supposition so extraordinarily probable; it requires alone that we should not obstinately insist upon it and set it up as an established certainty, but that we should lend a willing ear to better and surer knowledge whenever it is offered.

Professor Tyndall, too, in his *Lectures on Light*, referring to the genesis of all scientific knowledge, says—

All our notions of nature, however exalted or however grotesque, have some foundations in experience. The notion of personal volition in nature had this basis. In the fury and the serenity of natural phenomena the savage saw the transcript of his own varying moods, and he accordingly ascribed these phenomena to beings of like passions with himself, but vastly transcending him in power. Thus the notion of *causality*—the assumption that natural things did not come of themselves, but had unseen antecedents—lay at the root of even the savage's interpretation of nature. Out of this bias of the human mind to seek for the antecedents of phenomena, all science has sprung.

The value of "comparative folk-lore," in the elucidation of obscure passages in the early history of mankind, especially with regard to manners, customs, and superstitious faiths, is now pretty generally acknowledged by archaeological students. Since this chapter was first written I find the subject has been ably treated by Mr. J. A. Farrer, in the *Cornhill Magazine* of January, 1875. He says—

The evidence that the nations now highest in culture were once in the position of those now the lowest is ever increasing, and the study of folk-lore corroborates the conclusions long since arrived at by archaeological science. For, just as stone monuments, flint-knives, lake-piles, and shell-mounds point to a time when Europeans resembled races where such things are still part of actual life, so do the traces in our social organism, of fetishism, *totemism*, and other low forms of thought, connect our past with people where such forms of thought are still predominant. The analogies with barbarism that still flourish in civilised communities seem only explicable on the theory of a slow and more or less uniform metamorphosis to higher types and modes of life, and we are forced to believe that ere long it will appear a law of development, as firmly established on the inconceivability of the contrary, that civilization should emerge from barbarism as that butterflies should first be caterpillars, or that ignorance should precede knowledge. It is in this way that superstition itself may be turned to the service of science.

CHAPTER 3

Battles in the Valley of the Ribble, Near Whalley and Clitheroe

The *Anglo-Saxon Chronicle*, under the date 798, says—

This year there was a great fight at Hwelleage (Whalley), in the land of the Northumbrians, during Lent, on the 4th before the Nones of April, and there Alric, the son of Herbert, was slain, and many others with him.

Simeon of Durham has the following reference to this battle:—

A.D. 798. A conspiracy having been organised by the murderers of Ethelred, the king, Wada, the chief of that conspiracy, commenced a war against Eardulph, and fought a battle at a place called by the English Billangahoh, near Walalega, and, after many had fallen on both sides, Wada and his army were totally routed.

The Anglo-Saxon Chronicle informs us that four years previously (794), "Ethelred, king of the Northumbrians, was slain by his own people, on the 13th before the Kalends of May." This Ethelred seems to have been a very unfortunate or a very tyrannical ruler, even for those barbarous times, for we find, on the same authority, he, in company with Herbert, "slew three high reves, on the 11th before the *Kalends* of April," 778, and that afterwards "Alfwold obtained the kingdom, and drove Ethelred out of the country; and he (Alfwold) reigned ten years."

This same Alfwold was evidently regarded as a patriot and not as an usurper, for the *Chronicle* tells us that he "was slain by Siga, on the 8th before the *Kalends* of October; and a heavenly light was frequently

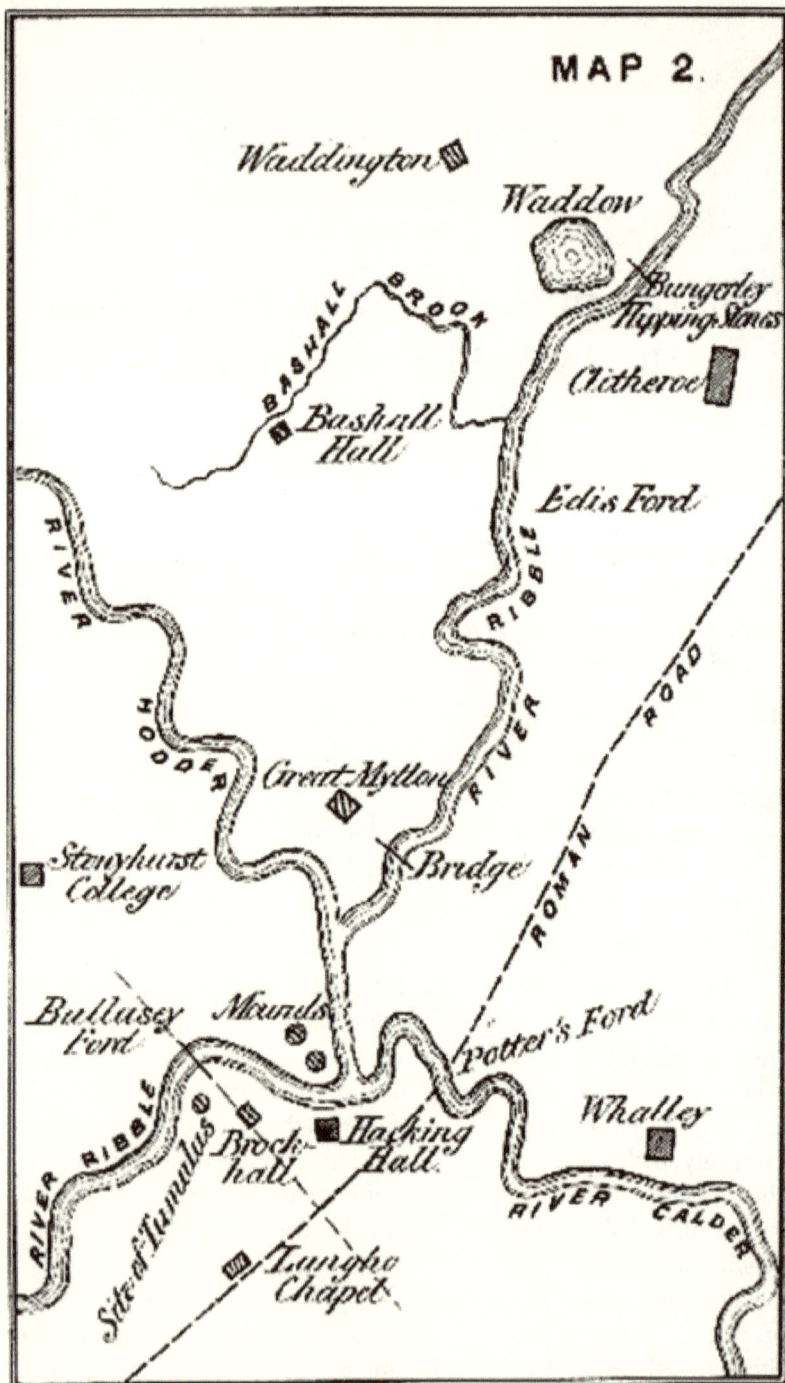

MAP 2.

seen at the place where he was slain; and he was buried at Hexham within the church." He was succeeded by his nephew, Osred, who, the *Chronicle* says, afterwards "was betrayed and driven from the kingdom; and Ethelred, the son of Ethelwald, again obtained the government." Two years later, from the same authority, we learn that "Osred, who had been king of the Northhumbrians, having come home from his exile, was seized and slain on the 18th before the Kalends of October," (792).

These facts throw much light on the social and political state of the country at the period, and demonstrate that Ethelred's murder was by no means an exceptional occurrence. Indeed, the slaying of kings by their own people appears to have been the rule rather than the exception amongst our ancestors, especially in Northumbria, about this period. Sharon-Turner, in his *History of the Anglo-Saxons*, referring to the internecine conflicts which took place in the North of England for a lengthened period, and especially about this time, says—

> Of all the Anglo-Saxon Governments the kingdom of North-umbria had been always the most perturbed. Usurper mur-dering usurper is the prevailing incident. A crowd of ghastly monarchs pass swiftly along the page of history as we gaze, and scarcely was the sword of the assassin sheathed before it was drawn against its master, and he was carried to the sepulchre which he had just closed upon another. In this manner, dur-ing the last century and a half, no fewer than seventeen scept-ered chiefs hurled each other from their joyless thrones, and the deaths of the greatest number were accompanied by hecatombs of their friends.

The public mind, under such circumstances, must of necessity have been deeply perturbed, and superstition associated the social and po-litical anarchy which prevailed with the "war of elements," and other attendant mysterious physical phenomena. The trusty old chronicler, duly impressed with the solemnity of his theme, informs us that dur-ing the year preceding the murder of Ethelred:

> Dire forewarnings came over the land of the Northumbrians and miserably terrified the people; these were excessive whirl-winds and lightnings, and fiery dragons were seen flying in the air. A great famine soon followed these tokens; and a little after that, in the same year, on the 6th before the *Ides* of January, the ravaging of heathen men lamentably destroyed God's Church

at Lindisfarne through rapine and slaughter.

The "heathen men" here referred to were Danish rovers. These "Northmen, out of Hæretha-land" (Denmark), had a few years previously (787), in three ships, "first sought the land of the English nation," and, having found it and pronounced it good, they ceased not their invasions until they became masters of the entire kingdom, under Canute the Great. This conquest of the Northmen mainly resulted from the fact that the English monarchs of the Heptarchy were continually at war either with the Britons or amongst themselves. "Domestic treason and fierce civil strife" added additional strength to the foe, for both regal enemy and rebellious subject eagerly sought the aid of the pirates, or selected the occasion of their hostile visits to harass their opponents. Although we have no record of Danish or other Northmen's ravages in Lancashire in the reign of Ethelred or his successor, yet we get a very distinct view of their doings on the eastern coast of Northumbria, and of the internecine strife which rendered the kingdom a relatively easy prey to the brave but brutal and remorseless heathen pirates.

The battles described in the previous chapters were more or less conjectural in some of their aspects; at least the true character of the presumed Arthurian victories on the Douglas, as well as the site of that of Penda over St. Oswald, at Maserfield, have not been demonstrated with such certainty as to obtain universal assent. Such, however, is not the case with the minor struggle now under consideration. The site assigned to it has never been doubted. The names recorded by the old chroniclers are still extant in the locality, with such orthographic or phonetic changes in their descent from the eighth to the nineteenth century as philologists would anticipate. The *Hwelleage* of the *Anglo-Saxon Chronicle,* as well as the monk of Durham's medieval Latin *Walalega*, are identical with the present Whalley; while *Billangahoh* is represented by its descendants Billinge, Billington, and Langho. Archæological remains have likewise contributed important evidence.

Three large *tumuli* for centuries have marked the scene of the struggle, one of which, near to Langho, has been removed, and the remains of a buried warrior exhumed. According to J. M. Kemble and other Anglo-Saxon scholars, Billington signifies the homestead or settlement of the sept or clan of the Billings, as Birmingham is that of the Beormings. This rule likewise applies to many other localities where the local nomenclature presents similar features. Consequently, from legitimate analogy, we learn that Waddington, on the right bank of the Ribble opposite Clitheroe, is the homestead, town, or settlement of Wadda and his dependents; and Waddow, in its immediate neighbourhood, the how or hill of Wadda.

In the fragment of the old Anglo-Saxon poem *The Traveller's Tale,* mention is made of a Wada as a chief of the Hælsings. Mr. Haigh, in his *Anglo-Saxon Sagas,* regards him as "probably one of the companions of the first Hencgest." Hence the probability of his being an ancestor of the chief conspirator against King Eardulph. Mr. Kemble (*Saxons in England,*) says—

> Among the heroes of heathen tradition are Wada, Weland, and Eigil. All three so celebrated in the mythus and epos of Scandinavia and Germany, have left traces in England. Of Wada, the *Traveller's Song* declares that he ruled the Hælsings; and even later times had to tell of Wade's *boat,* in which the exact allusion is unknown to us: the Scandinavian story makes him wade across the Groenasund, carrying his son across his shoulder. Perhaps our tradition gives a different version of this story.

This story may have something to do with the genesis of the legend of St. Christopher bearing the infant Christ on his shoulders over a broad stream, a subject of one of the early medieval pictures discovered some time ago, on the removal of the whitewash from the walls of Gawsworth Church, near Macclesfield. The historical anachronism in ascribing such an action to him may have resulted from the mere transference of it from the pagan hero to the Christian saint. The original story seems to have been pretty familiar to the people as late as the fourteenth century. Mr. Kemble says—

> Chaucer once or twice refers to this (Wade's *boat*) in such a way as to show that the expression was used in an obscene sense. Old women, he says, 'connen so moche craft in Wade's boat.' Again of Pandarus:
>
> *He song, he plaied, he told a tale of Wade.*
> > Troil. Cressid.
>
> 'In this there seems to be some allusion to what anatomists have termed *fossa navicularis,* though what immediate connection there could be with the mythical Wade, now escapes us.'

The *Traveller's Tale* likewise refers to a chieftain named "Billing," who "ruled the Wærns," and who, in Mr. Haigh's opinion, was likewise a "probable associate of Hencgest." Mr. Haigh likewise identifies Whaley in Cheshire, Whalley in Northumberland, and Whalley in Lancashire, with a chieftain described in the same poem as "Hwala once the best." Dr. Whitaker, Mr. Baines, and others, however, derive Whalley from *Walalega*, "Field of Wells."

Mr. Jno. R. Green (*Making of England*,) says—

In the star-strown track of the Milky Way, our fathers saw a road by which the hero-sons of Waetla marched across the sky, and poetry only hardened into prose when they transferred the name of Watling Street to the great trackway which passed athwart the island they had won, from London to Chester. The stones of Weyland's Smithy still recall the days when the new settlers told one another, on the conquered ground, the wondrous tale they had brought with them from their German home, the tale of the godlike smith Weland, who forged the arms that none could blunt or break; just as they told around Wadanbury and Wadanhlæw the strange tale of Wade and his boats. When men christened mere and tree with Scyld's name, at Scyldsmere and Styldstreow, they must have been familiar with the story of the godlike child who came over the waters to found the royal line of the Gwissas. So a name like Hnaef's-scylf was then a living part of English mythology; and a name like Aylesbury may preserve the last trace of the legend told of Weland's brother, the sun-archer Egil.

Although we possess but little information respecting the details of the fight, or of the political complications out of which it arose, we are, at least, perfectly certain of the locality of the struggle. In addition, the magnificent scenery by which it is surrounded, in which grandeur and beauty are seen in the most harmonious combination, the interesting archaeological remains, and the numerous other historic associations of the neighbourhood, including those connected with Whalley Abbey, Clitheroe Castle, Mytton, and Stonyhurst, give an interest to the locality which is denied to the sites of many battlefields, the names of which have become "household words," not merely with one nation or people, but with all the so-called civilised section of mankind.

One of the *tumuli* to which I have referred was partially opened by Dr. T. D. Whitaker, the historian of Whalley. But, as in his day Anglo-Saxon antiquities were very little sought after and, consequently, very imperfectly understood, his labours were productive of nothing but negative results. Canon Raines, however, in a note to his edition of the *Notitia Cestriensis*, published by the Chetham Society, says—

> In the year 1836, as Thomas Hubbertsty, the farmer at Brockhall, was removing a large mound of earth in Brockhall Eases, about five hundred yards from the bank of the Ribble, on the left of the road leading from the house, he discovered a Kist-vaen, formed of rude stones, containing some human bones and the rusty remains of some spear-heads of iron. The whole crumbled to dust on exposure to the air. Tradition has uniformly recorded that a battle was fought about Langho, Elker and Buckfoot, near the Ribble; and a *tumulus* was opened within two hundred yards of a ford of the Ribble (now called Bullasey-ford), one of the very few points for miles where that river could be crossed. The late Dr. Whitaker repeatedly, but in vain, searched for remains of this battle, as he appears to have erroneously concluded that the scene of it was higher up the river, near Hacking Hall, at the junction of the Calder and the Ribble.

Dr. Whitaker does not appear to have noticed all the tumuli in the neighbourhood. In his *History of Whalley* he says—

> Of this great battle there are no remains, unless *a large tumulus* near Hacking Hall, and in the immediate vicinity of Langho, be supposed to cover the remains of Alric, or some other chieftain among the slain.

The site of the *tumulus*, on the left bank, or south-east side of the Ribble, is marked on the Ordnance map. It is scarcely three quarters of a mile from Hacking Hall, and rather more than a mile from Langho chapel. No other *tumulus* is noticed by the Ordnance surveyors on the south-east side of the river.

Canon Raines states that the "large mound" removed by Thomas Hubbertsty, in 1836, was situated "about five hundred yards from the bank of the Ribble," and that the *tumulus* that had been previously opened was only two hundred yards distant from that stream. The "large mound" of Canon Raines, removed in 1836, in which remains were found, seems to have been a smaller affair than the other *tumuli*. This is affirmed by Mr. Abram, in a very able paper on the history of the township of Billington, in the *Lancashire and Cheshire Historical Society's Transactions,* otherwise he says, "the farmer would hardly have undertaken to level it." The *tumuli* on the right bank or north-west side of the river are named "lowes" on the six-inch Ordnance map, and "mounds" on the smaller one. The former name is evidently the Anglo-Saxon *hlœw*, a conical hill or a sepulchral mound, or tumulus, in the latter sense a synonym of *beorh* or *bearw*, a barrow. Although these large tumuli are on the north-west side of the river, the nearest is scarcely half a mile distant from the site of the removed one near Bullasey-ford on the south-east.

There is some confusion in the various descriptions of these mounds. Mr. Abram says, referring to the large tumulus called the "Lowe" on the north-west side of the Ribble—

> Into this mound Whitaker had some excavation made about the year 1815, but he found the work heavy and gave it up without reaching the centre of the *tumulus*, where the relics of sepulture might be expected to be found.

As Dr. Whitaker expressly says, he saw no remains of the battle except "a large *tumulus* near Hacking Hall," he must not only have been ignorant of the character of its immediate neighbour, as well as of the one on the Langho side of the river, near Bullasey-ford, if this "lowe" was the mound he but partially disturbed. This can scarcely be the tumulus referred to by Canon Raines if the distance (two hundred yards) from the river be correct. Neither can the five hundred yards distance of Mr. Hubbertsty's mound be reconciled with the site of the *tumulus* at Brockhall, near Bullasey-ford. Perhaps his figures have been accidently transposed. I had previously laboured under an impression that Hubbertsty had merely completely cleared away the mound but imperfectly excavated by Dr. Whitaker.

Being anxious to arrive at some more definite knowledge respecting these "lowes" or "mounds," on the ninth of Nov., 1876, I visited the locality, and by the aid of Mr. Parkinson, the present tenant of Brockhall, I was enabled to make a far more detailed inspection of the battlefield than on a hurried visit about twenty years previously. Mr. Parkinson pointed out the site of the *tumulus* removed by Mr. Hub-bertsty in 1836. Nothing of it, of course, now remains. He said that it was the only mound of the kind he had ever heard of on the Langho side of the Ribble. He, however, pointed out a curious circular *agger*, about five or six feet broad and a couple of feet high, which enclosed a level area some sixteen or seventeen yards in diameter.

It is evidently an artificial work, but without additional evidence it is impossible to say, with any reasonable degree of probability, by whom it was constructed, or to what use it was originally applied. On the steep promontory called "Brockhole Wood-end," Mr. Parkinson called my attention to curious masses of cemented sand and pebble stones, which some persons regarded as artificial grout, that had originally formed part of the massive masonry of an ancient building, the foundations of which had been undermined by the falling in of the earth in consequence of the erosive action of the flood water of the Ribble at the base of the cliff.

This, however, I found, on examination, to be erroneous. The "grout" in question is a geological phenomenon, a kind of conglomerate or *breccia*, formed by the percolation of rain water, charged with carbonic acid and lime, through the mass of glacial or boulder "till" and its sandy and pebbly contents. The "till" contains limestones brought by ice from both the Ribble and the Hodder valleys. The phenomenon is a common one to geologists, and the "concrete" at "Brockhole Wood-end" is an excellent example of it. On gazing across the river at the larger "lowe" of the six-inch Ordnance map, Mr. Parkinson remarked that it appeared to him to be what is termed by geologists an outlier of the boulder deposits on each side of the valley, and therefore, not an artificial mound. He pointed out that the flood waters of the Ribble, Hodder, and Calder met in the plain, and when the "till" was excavated by a kind of circular motion of the combined waters, which the present appearance of the valley indicates, the land situated in the centre or vortex would the longer resist the abrading action, and eventually, as the passage of the currents became enlarged, remain a surviving outlier of the general mass of glacial deposit.

On passing the river in the ferry-boat, and, by the aid of a pickaxe, exposing the material of which this mound is formed, I confessed that I could detect no difference in its character or structure from that of the neighbouring geological deposits. Still, as the mound, if artificial, must have been constructed from the boulder clay and its unstratified contents, this is not surprising. It is, however, impossible to solve this problem without a much more searching investigation. Even if a mound existed at the time the battle was fought, nothing is more probable than that it would be utilised by the victors in the interment of their honoured dead.

The second and smaller mound seems very like an artificial one; but this cannot be satisfactorily affirmed without more complete investigation. Both mounds have been partially opened near their summits, but with only negative results, as might have been anticipated, as the Christian Anglo-Saxons in such cases buried the body in the earth, and afterwards heaped the tumulus or barrow above it, as a monument to the memory of the deceased warrior or warriors. This mode of interment had been adopted in the instance of the tumulus removed by Mr. Hubbertsty in 1836.

Interesting results, both to geologists and archaeologists, may, therefore, be anticipated from a thorough examination of the contents of these remarkable "lowes" or "mounds;" but, as some expense would be attendant thereupon, they may yet, for some time, remain an interesting puzzle, both to the learned and the unlearned in such matters. They are situated in the midst of the level alluvial plain. The largest is nearly twenty feet high, and forms a prominent object.

When I first visited the locality I was much amused at the rough and ready way in which some of the country people accounted for their construction, or rather the object thereof. They had seen sheep, when the Ribble valley was flooded, mount on the top of them for safety, and they innocently concluded that these historic monuments, mementoes of deadly civil strife during the eighth century, or of the glacial period of geologists, had been erected by some benevolent or thrifty ancestor of the owner of the soil for the especial accommodation of ovine refugees during the deluges to which the low-lying land on the margin of the river is occasionally subjected.

It is, of course, at the present time, impossible to define the extent of ground covered by the contending armies during the conflict, or to give even a satisfactory outline of the general features of the battle. The Roman road, the seventh *iter* of Richard of Cirencester, which leads from the Wyre (the Portus Setantiorum of Ptolemy), by Preston and Ribchester to York, passed through the township of Billington, crossed the Calder near the present "Potter's Ford," a little above its junction with the Ribble, and proceeded a little south of Clitheroe and north of Pendle-hill, by Standen Hall, and Worston, in Lancashire, and Downham, into Yorkshire. Mr. Abram seems to think that the battle was most probably fought on this line of road. He says—

> Eardulf encountered the insurgent army on the extreme verge
> of his kingdom (for it seems certain that the country south
> of the Ribble was then a part, not of the Saxon kingdom of
> Northumbria, but that of Mercia). Wada and his army had prob-
> ably been driven upon the neutral territory before the decisive

battle could be forced upon him.

This notion that the Ribble and not the Mersey was the southern boundary of Northumbria in the earlier period of the Heptarchy, was first propounded by Dr. Whitaker, but upon very slight evidence. It is sufficient here to say that the Anglo-Saxon Chronicle, under the date 923, expressly states that King Edward sent a force of Mercians to take possession of "Mameceastre (Manchester), *in Northumbria*, and repair and man it." Again, the same chronicle, when referring to this very battle, *A.D.* 798, expressly states that it took place "at Whalley, *in the land of the Northumbrians.*"

Against such evidence, Dr. Whitaker's mistaken dialectal argument, as well as that based on the extent of the episcopal see of Lichfield, at some period of the Heptarchy, is utterly valueless. His authority is the ancient document entitled *De Statu Blackborneshire*, supposed to have been written in the fourteenth century by John Lindeley, Abbot of Whalley. Some notion of the value of this monkish compilation, with reference to the earlier history of the district, may be gathered from the fact that the author makes Augustine, and not Paulinus, the missionary who planted Christianity amongst the Northumbrian Angles. Dr. Whitaker likewise contends that the Ribble is the *dialectic* boundary between the two kingdoms. My own observation, however, leads me to a very different conclusion. To my ear the change is by no means so distinctly marked on the north and south sides of the Ribble as it is on the north and south banks of the Mersey.

The swampy country between the two rivers would rather seem to have been a kind of "march" or "debateable ground," during the earlier portion of the Anglo-Saxon and Danish periods, districts in it being sometimes governed by tributary British chieftains under both Northumbrian and Mercian kings as the fortune of war from time to time prevailed. Lancashire is not referred to as a county till the middle of the twelfth century. The name is never mentioned in the Anglo-Saxon Chronicle. As we find the "Lands between the Ribble and the Mersey" are surveyed with those of Cheshire, in the Domesday book, it seems highly probable that they formed a part of Leofric's earldom of Mercia, at the time of the Norman conquest. Consequently it is to the latter and not to the earlier portion of the Anglo-Saxon period that the Ribble formed the southern boundary of the *earldom* of Northumbria, rather than of the earlier independent *kingdom*.

Mr. J. R. Green (*Making of England,*) says—

The first missionaries to the Englishmen, strangers in a heathen land, attached themselves necessarily to the courts of the kings, who were their earliest converts, and whose conversion was generally followed by that of their people. The English bishops were thus at first royal chaplains, and their diocese was naturally nothing but the kingdom. The kingdom of Kent became the diocese of Canterbury, and the kingdom of Northumbria became the diocese of York. So absolutely was this the case that the diocese grew or shrank with the growth or shrinking of the realm which it spiritually represented, and a bishop of Wessex or of Mercia found the limits of his see widened or cut short by the triumphs of Wolfhere or of Ine. In this way two realms, which are all but forgotten, are commemorated in the limits of existing sees. That of Rochester represented, till of late, an obscure kingdom of West Kent, and the frontier of the original kingdom of Mercia might be recovered by following the map of the ancient bishopric of Lichfield.

After describing in detail some of the subdivisions made by Archbishop Theodore (*A.D.* 669-672), he adds—

"The see of Lichfield thus returned to its original form of a see of the Mercians proper, though its bounds on the westward now embraced much of the upper Severn valley, with Cheshire and the lands northward to the Mersey."

Notwithstanding this error with regard to the southern boundary of Northumbria at that period, the Roman road, in all probability, was utilised by the contending forces, and some portion of the main battle was, doubtless, fought in its immediate vicinity. On the other hand, it is equally probable, as the two larger tumuli are situated on the north-west bank of the Ribble, that the chief conflict occurred in their neighbourhood. On this hypothesis, Wada and his allies, on leaving Waddington, crossed the Hodder, at the ford nearest its mouth, met the King's army on the banks of the Ribble, and the possession of Bullasey-ford was the immediate object of the encounter in which the rebellious chieftain was discomfited. Or the route may have been reversed.

Wada may have crossed the Ribble, at the Bungerley "hyppyngstones," to the north-west of Clitheroe, or the Edisford, to the south-west, and after penetrating the southern portion of the present county, had to fall back before the advance of the King's army, and, unable to retrace his steps he made for the nearer ford at Bullasey, where he was defeated and pursued across the river. As the slaughter is generally greater when a discomfited enemy is routed, perhaps the two large tumuli, named "lowes," mark the spot where the greatest carnage ensued. This, however, of course, is merely conjecture. Its value cannot be tested unless a thorough investigation of the contents of these huge mounds should throw additional light upon the subject.

The good fortune of King Eardulf deserted him on a future occasion. The *Anglo-Saxon Chronicle* says—

> *A.D. 806.* This year the moon was eclipsed in the *Kalends* of September; and Eardulf, King of the Northhumbrians, was driven from his kingdom. . . . Also in the same year, on the 2nd before the *Nones* of June, a cross appeared in the moon on a Wednesday at dawn; and afterwards in this year, on the 3rd before the *Kalends* of September, a wonderful circle was seen about the sun.

This is the last we hear of the victor of Billangahoh, and the manner of his exit from the historic stage would seem to indicate that his rule, like that of his predecessor, had become so intolerable that further revolts ensued, and that Wada's successors, whoever they may have been, being successful in their contumacy, would be regarded, not as traitors, but as "saviours of their country." Truly, in struggles of this character, in all ages, successful "rebels," writing their own history, are ever lauded as heroes or patriots, while discomfited rulers are, with equal verity, denounced as tyrants and enemies of the common weal.

A little higher up the Ribble than its junction with the Hodder, and about a mile below the venerable ruin of the keep of Clitheroe Castle, the ancient stronghold of the De Lacies, is a handsome modern bridge, named Edisford or Eadsford, to which I have previously referred. The country people, however, call it "Itch-uth Bridge," pronouncing the latter syllable as in Cuthburt.

Johannes, Prior of Hagulstald, records that in this neighbourhood, in the year 1138, one William, the son of the bastard brother of David, king of Scotland, when engaged on a foray into England, was gallantly encountered by a small band, near Clitheroe, but, being overpowered by numbers, the Lancashire men sustained a slight defeat, and the Scots took a considerable number of prisoners. The monkish chronicler calls the northern assailants "Picts and Scots," and adds that they with difficulty held their own till the fight had lasted three hours.

Tradition has preserved both the memory and the site of this conflict. Mr. Edward Baines says:—

Vestiges of this sanguinary engagement have been found at Edisford Bridge, and along the banks of the Ribble, during successive ages up to the present time.

The "Bashall-brook," after passing "Bashall Hall," enters the Ribble a little above Edisford Bridge. This is the stream referred to by Mr. Haigh,[1] as the "Bassus" of Nennius, and the site of one of the Arthurian victories which attended Colgrin's flight to York, after his defeat on the Douglas, near Wigan. I have, however, never heard of any legend or tradition which referred to a battle in the neighbourhood, except the one recorded by the Prior of Hagulstald.

Near the bridge above Clitheroe may yet be seen the ancient "hyppyngstones" to which I have previously referred, and by means of which the river was crossed before the erection of the present viaduct. These "hyppyngstones" have at least one mournful historical association. After the fatal Battle of Hexham, in the year 1464, the unfortunate Henry the Sixth, the defeated son of the renowned victor at Agincourt, was for a time concealed at Bolton-in-Bolland and Waddington Halls. What transpired is best told in the words of the old chronicler:—

Also the same yere, Kinge Henry was taken byside a howse of religione (*i.e.*, Whalley Abbey) in Lancashyre, by the mene of a blacke monke of Abyngtone, in a wode called Cletherwode, beside Bungerley hyppyngstones, by Thomas Talbott, of Bashalle, and Jhon Talbott, his cosyne, of Colebury (*i.e.*, Salesbury, near Ribchester), with other moo; which discryvide (him) beynge at his dynere at Waddington Hall; and (he was) carryed to London on horsebacke, and his legges bound to the styropes.[2]

Mr. J. G. Nichols (*Notes and Queries*, vol 2., p. 229), says—

Waddington belonged to Sir John Tempest, of Bracewell, who was the father-in-law to Thomas Talbot. Both Sir John Tempest and Sir James Harrington, of Brierley, near Barnsley, were concerned in the king's capture, and each received one hundred marks reward, but the fact of Sir Thomas Talbot being the chief actor, is shown by his having received the large sum of £100.

1. See Chapter 1.
2. *Warksworth Chronicle.*

In addition to his one hundred *marks*, Sir James Harrington received from Edward IV. large grants of land, forfeited by Richard Tunstell, and other "rebels," "for his services in taking prisoner, and withholding as such, in diligence and valour, his enemy, Henry, lately called Henry VI." Mr. Baines says:

> Sir John Talbot likewise received as a reward for his perfidy, a grant of twenty *marks* a year, from Edward IV., confirmed by his successor, Richard III., and made payable out of the revenues of the county palatine of Lancaster.

In his *History of Craven*, Dr. Whitaker gives engravings of the unfortunate monarch's boots, gloves, and a spoon, which were preserved at Bolton Hall, in Bolland, Yorkshire, then the seat of Sir Ralph Pudsey, who married a daughter of Sir Thomas Tunstell. I understand these relics of the unfortunate king have been since removed to Hornby Castle, Lancashire. The "Old Hall" at Waddington, which has been converted into a farmhouse, yet presents some massive masonry, and a field in the neighbourhood still retains the name of "King Henry's meadow."

The fate of the unhappy monarch is too well known to necessitate further reference here.

The neighbourhood of Whalley was the scene of a relatively more recent combat, of some local importance. During the civil war between Charles I. and his Parliament, the Earl of Derby advanced, in 1643, from Preston, to operate in the hundred of Blackburn. One of the *Civil War Tracts*, edited by Ormerod, and published by the Chetham Society, says:—

> The Earl of Derby, the Lord Molineux, Sir Gilbert Hoghton, Colonel Tildesley, with all the other great papists in the county, issued out of Preston, and on Wednesday now came to Ribchester, with eleven troops of horse, 700 foot, and an infinite number of clubmen, in all conceived to be 5,000.

Colonels Ashton and Shuttleworth opposed them with some regular troops, and a body of peasantry and militia, hastily levied. A regular engagement, or rather a running fight, took place between Whalley and Salesbury, in which the Earl was defeated and pursued to Ribchester. This success appears to have been the precursor of the subsequent declension of the Earl of Derby's military power in the county. It was judged to be of so much importance at the time by the

"Roundheads," that a day of thanksgiving was set apart for the victory by order of Parliament.

The ruin of Clitheroe Castle, on its well-wooded limestone eminence overlooking the town, forms a picturesque object in the beautiful valley of the Ribble. I remember well, in my early boyhood, being seriously informed that the venerable feudal stronghold of the De Lacies was battered into ruin by no less a personage than the redoubtable Oliver Cromwell. The truth of this tradition was implicitly believed by me till some slight study of Lancashire history, and a special visit to the locality, threw serious doubt upon it. I have likewise a distinct recollection of the consternation I caused amongst some aged friends, after a careful inspection of the ruined keep, by my informing them that if, as the tradition asserted, Cromwell had placed his cannon on "Salt Hill," about a mile to the east of the fortress, the said ordnance must have possessed some of the marvellous property ascribed to the Hibernian weapon, which, on occasion, could "shoot round a corner," the wall of the keep presenting the largest amount of superficial damage facing directly west.

This dilapidated aspect had, in my hearing, often been attributed to the pounding the wall had received from Oliver's cannon. A careful examination, however, satisfied me that the western face of the structure was simply most weather-worn, on account of the lengthened action of the prevailing south-westerly winds. Again, "Salt Hill" was too far distant for the eight-pounder field pieces of the parliamentary army to make any serious impression on the massive walls.[3] But tradition is "tough" indeed, and especially if an element of superstition or partisan zeal be embedded in it. Of course, my critics had not the slightest objection to allow that there might possibly be some mistake with regard to the site of his guns, but "everybody knew that Cromwell did batter the castle into ruin," notwithstanding; and I was frankly told that nobody thanked me for my *mischievous* endeavour to undermine people's faith in the well-known legend!

Cromwell must certainly have *seen* Clitheroe Castle on his memorable forced march from Gisburne to Stonyhurst Hall, on August 16th, 1648, the day previous to his decisive victory over the Marquis of Langdale, on Ribbleton Moor, and the Duke of Hamilton at Preston

---

3. Several cannon balls, fired during Cromwell's military operations in this short but decisive campaign, have been found in the neighbourhood of Ribbleton, Ashton, and Walton-le-dale. They are about eight pounds weight each. One of them is in my possession at the present time.

and the "Pass of the Ribble." But there are two good and sufficient reasons why he did not stay to expend his gunpowder on the fortress. In the first place, he had not time, having important business on hand that demanded the utmost expedition. In the second place, the castle was garrisoned by a portion of the Lancashire Militia, who held the stronghold for the Parliament, and Cromwell was not the man to amuse himself by bombarding his friends on the eve of a great, and, as it proved, a decisive battle.

In point of fact, the castle remained intact, till the end of the civil war, when the only recorded instance of its ever having been even seriously threatened with a siege, occurred. An ordinance, disbanding the militia generally throughout the country, did not, it seems, meet with the approval of the Puritan warriors who held possession of the Clitheroe fortress, and who, instigated, it was said, by clerical advisers, "professed for the Covenant," and, in the first instance, flatly refused to disband until their terms were accepted. After the enforcement of the law, however, had been entrusted to Major-General Lambert, these chivalrous champions of the Covenant thought, under such circumstances, discretion was unquestionably the better part of valour, and they surrendered the castle to the Parliamentary general without further pressure.

By an order of a Council of State, several of these strongholds throughout the country were dismantled, with a view to prevent their military occupation in case of a renewal of the war, and amongst those so doomed were the castles of Clitheroe and Greenhaugh, in the county of Lancaster. Thus ignominiously expires one element in the presumed historic truth of Cromwell's numerous castle and abbey battering exploits, referred to at length in the first chapter of this work, and on which the most remarkable and wide-spread legend of *modern* and strictly historic times is based.

A still more astounding instance of the appropriation of popular legends and famous names by localities that have no historical claims to them whatever, is found in connection with the ancient castle at Bury, Lancashire. Mr. Edward Baines says—

In the civil wars which raged in Lancashire in 1644, Bury Castle was battered by the Parliamentary army from an intrenchment called 'Castle-steads,' in the adjoining township of Walmersley; and from that period the overthrow of this, as well as of a large proportion of other castles of the kingdom, may be dated.

Mr. Baines gives no authority whatever for this astounding statement. He evidently merely repeats a well-known local tradition. It would have been worth the while of a local historian, one would think, to have made some enquiry as to the history of the edifice at Bury during the century which had elapsed between Leland's reference to it, and the redoubtable exploit of the Parliamentary army in 1644. The earliest authentic record of the castle is no older than the reign of Henry VIII., but from the very nature of the record it must have been in existence for a long time previously. Leland, the "king's antiquary," when travelling through the country "in search of England's antiquities," *circa* 1542-9, thus writes about the place—

> Byri-on-Irwell, 4 or 5 miles from Manchestre, but a poore market. There is a Ruine of a Castel by the paroch chirch yn the Towne. It longgid with the Towne sumetime to the Pilkentons, now to the Erles of Darby. Pilkenton had a place hard by Pilkenton Park, 3 miles from Manchestre.

Leland's distances are, of course, merely guesses. In this respect he is frequently in error. It is certain that the de Bury family held land in the parish as recently as 1613, and we find the manorial rights, at the time of the "Wars of the Roses," were held by the Pilkington family. Sir Thomas Pilkington, a devoted adherent to the fortunes of the House of York, obtained from Edward IV. a licence to "kernel and embattle" his manor-home at Stand, in Pilkington. It is not, therefore, improbable that the Bury castle at this time ceased to be a manorial residence, and gradually fell into the ruinous condition in which it was seen by Leland.

During the time I was inspecting the excavation by the local commissioners of the site of Bury castle, in October, 1865, I was courteously permitted by Mr. J. Shaw, of that town, to copy a MS., formerly the property of his late father, and, I understood, in that gentleman's handwriting. It is, however, dated "Bury, April 13th, 1840," and signed "T. Crompton," or "Krompton," it is difficult to determine which. As the document may be said to embody all the "traditional lore" respecting the subject under consideration, I give it entire:—

> Bury in the Olden Time, or the Siege of the Castle, etc.
> Bury Castle, supposed to be built in the reign of Richard II., in 1380. The date when erected cannot be positively ascertained. The coin of the Stuarts, etc., have been found in the foundations. The whole of the castle was destroyed by the Parliamen-

tary arms, in 1642-3, when the wars between Charles I. and Cromwell deluged poor England in the blood of her own children. Edward de Bury was attached to the unfortunate Charles's cause. He fell, with many others, a prey to the party spirit then raging so horribly in the land. The River Irwell passed by the north side of the castle, and run by the north-east turret, the site of the castle, which forms a parallelogram, was about 11 roods square, and from the foundation (the walls) seem to have been about two yards thick, with four round towers, about 60 feet high each. A large stone has been found which belonged to the archway, with the arms of De Bury engraved thereon. This drama [*sic*] is principally taken from a legendary tale of Bury Castle. Cromwell's army (by Stanley) was placed on Bury Moor. The cannon in an intrenchment at Castle Head [*sic*] on the Walmesley side of the river. Lord Strange arrayed his army of 20,000 for the Royal cause on Gallow's Hill, Tottington Side. The river opposite the Castle, before the course was altered, was about 100 to 120 yards wide.

Traditionary lore, though on the whole generally founded on some fact or facts, which have become distorted, owing to their frequent oral transmission by persons utterly ignorant of their original signification, is scarcely ever to be relied on so far as individuals or dates are concerned. The stories do unquestionably attest the retention in the popular mind of something of import that took place in that vague period denominated the "olden time," but not always accurately what that *something* may have been. The Adam de Bury referred to in the document quoted is either a myth, or the name has reference to some earlier individual interested in the castle at Bury. Indeed the family appears to have become extinct before the commencement of the civil wars referred to.

On this point the documentary evidence quoted by Mr. E. Baines is very conclusive. There can have been no "Adam de Bury attached to the unfortunate Charles's cause," or his name would have appeared amongst the Lancashire "lords, knights, and gentlemen," who compounded with the sequestration commissioners for their estates in 1646.

Cromwell's army could not have been placed on Bury Moor, by either Stanley or anyone else, in 1642-3, as that general did not enter Lancashire till 1648, and then his route lay by Stonyhurst, Preston, Wigan, and Warrington. Lord Strange's "army" of 20,000 men is but another form of expression for the public meeting held on Bury Moor, the numbers stated as attending which are doubtless much exaggerated. A similar meeting was held on Preston Moor, and, singularly enough, as it was a numerous one, the same authority employs the same terms—20,000—to express the fact. The placing of the cannon at Castle Stead is another proof of the ignorance of some of the transmitters of the tradition, the ordnance during Charles's time being useless at such a distance.

The statement in Mr. Shaw's document that "coin of the Stuarts, etc., have been found in the foundations," is valueless, inasmuch as until the excavations in 1865, the soil about the *foundations* does not appear to have been disturbed; and yet above the original surface, remains were found of various relatively modern dates, as might have been anticipated.

I have said there is generally some germ of truth at the bottom of this class of legendary stories. In this case it is not only possible but highly probable, that older traditions having reference to the "Wars of the Roses," may have been confounded with more recent events. This is by no means an uncommon occurrence, as I have previously contended. Singularly enough, Mr. Baines laments the lack of historical documents relating to Lancashire during this eventful period, and which he attributes to the wilful destruction to which they were subjected by the partisans of both the contending houses. The only historical event of any public interest recorded in connection with the bloody struggle for the crown of England between the Yorkists and the Lancastrians, relates to the capture of the unfortunate Henry VI. at "Bungerley hyppyngstones," previously referred to. It is therefore not improbable that some local events, lost to history, may have survived in the mutilated form in which tradition presents them at the present day, although their strictly historical significance is lost, and, what is worse, flagrant error has usurped its place in the popular mind.

It does not appear, on the authority of any trustworthy evidence, that Cromwell ever visited Lancashire, at least in a military capacity, except on the occasion of his great victory over Langdale and Hamilton in 1648. Of his movements immediately preceding that event, we have his own statement in a dispatch addressed to "The Honourable William Lenthall, Esquire, Speaker of the House of Commons." He says—

Hearing that the enemy was advanced with their army into Lancashire, we marched the next day, being the 13th of this instant August, to Otley (*having cast off our train*, and sent it to Knaresborough, because of the difficulty of marching therewith through Craven, and to the end that we might *with more expedition* attend the enemy's motion): and on the 14th to Skipton; the 15th to Gisburne; the 16th to Hodder Bridge, over Ribble; where we held a council of war, at which we had in consideration, whether we should march to Whalley that night, and so on, to interpose between the enemy and his further progress into Lancashire, and so southward,—which we had some advertisement the enemy intended, and (we are) since confirmed that they intended for London itself: or whether to march immediately over the said Bridge, there being no other betwixt that and Preston, and there engage the enemy,—who we did believe would stand his ground, because we had information that the Irish forces under Munro lately come out of Ireland, which consisted of twelve hundred horse and fifteen hundred foot, were on their march towards Lancashire to join them.

It was thought that to engage the enemy to fight was our business; and the reason aforesaid giving us hopes that our marching on the north side of Ribble would effect it, it was resolved we should march over the bridge, which accordingly we did, and that night quartered the whole army in the field by Stonyhurst Hall, being Mr. Sherburn's house, a place nine miles distant from Preston.[4] Very early the next morning we marched towards Preston, having intelligence that the enemy was drawing together thereabouts from all his out quarters.

At first sight it appears that Cromwell refers to some bridge which spanned the River Ribble, and named Hodder Bridge. This, however, is not the case. By the word "over" he means *beyond*, that is they passed over the Ribble to a bridge spanning the Hodder. Stonyhurst can be approached from the east by two bridges over this stream called the "upper" and the "lower." Both have been superseded by new structures, but some picturesque ruins of their predecessors yet remain. In a note at page 187, *History of Preston and its Environs*, I say—

As Cromwell's army advanced by way of Gisburn he would

---

4. This is an error, excusable under the circumstances. Stonyhurst is about twelve miles from Preston.

necessarily pass through Waddington to the higher bridge, over the River Hodder, on his route to Stonyhurst.

In this case he could ford the Ribble near Salley Abbey a few miles above Clitheroe, or at the Bungerley "hyppyngstones," nearer the town. From Cromwell's slight reference to Clitheroe, and his uncertainty respecting the troops occupying the place, together with Colonel Hodgson's reference to "Waddey," both of which will be again referred to, this is the most probable route. But from Gisburn, he *may* have come direct to Clitheroe, and, passing through the town, have crossed the Ribble at Eddisford a little below, and proceeded from thence to Stonyhurst by the "lower bridge of Hodder."

Further, in the evening after the battle, in a letter to the "Honourable Committee of Lancashire, sitting at Manchester," dated "Preston, 17th August, 1648," Cromwell expresses some uncertainty as to the forces stationed at Clitheroe, which evidently shows he made no stay in the immediate neighbourhood. He says—

> We understand Colonel-General Ashton's (forces) are at Whalley; we have seven troops of horse or dragoons that we *believe* lie at Clitheroe. This night I have sent order to them expressly to march to Whalley, to join to these companies; that so we may endeavour the ruin of the enemy.

Captain John Hodgson, of "Coalley," near Halifax, whom Thomas Carlyle somewhat unceremoniously and unnecessarily describes as an "honest-hearted, pudding-headed Yorkshire Puritan,"[5] left behind him a kind of journal, in which the details of the campaign are described with great clearness and minuteness. Hodgson, as his conduct shows, was not only an honest, but a brave and skilful soldier. He says—

> The next day we marched to Clitheroe; and at Waddey (Waddow, between Clitheroe and Waddington,) our forlorn of horse took Colonel Tempest and a party of horse, for an earnest of what was behind. That night we pitched our camp at Stanyares Hall, a Papist's house, one Sherburne; and the next morning

---

5. So savage a critic as Joseph Ritson seems to have entertained a much higher opinion of Captain Hodgson's literary qualities than the "seer of Chelsea." In his preface to the memoir he says—"Without meaning to dispute the merit of Defoe, in his peculiarly happy manner of telling a story, or, in other words, in the art of book-making, it will probably be found, that, truth or falsehood being out of the question, in point of importance, interest, and even pleasantry, Captain Hodgson's narrative is infinitely superior to the *Memoirs of a Cavalier.*"

a forlorn was drawn out of horse and foot; and, at Langridge Chapel, our horse gleaned up a considerable parcel of the enemy, and fought them all the way until within a mile of Preston.

If any military action, of even trifling importance, had taken place at Clitheroe it could not possibly have escaped the notice both of the general and his detail-loving "commander of the forlorn of foot." After describing the earlier portion of the struggle with Langdale's troops on Ribbleton moor, he says—

My captain sees me mounted[6] and orders me to ride up to my colonel, that was deeply engaged both in front and flank: and I did so, and there was nothing but fire and smoke; and I met Major-General Lambert coming off on foot, who had been with his brother Bright, and coming to him, I told him where his danger lay, on his left wing chiefly. He ordered me to fetch up the Lancashire regiment; and God brought me off, both horse and myself. The bullets flew freely; then was the heat of the battle that day. I came down to the muir, where I met with Major Jackson, that belonged to Ashton's regiment, and about three hundred men were come up; and I ordered him to march, but he said he would not, till his men were come up. A serjeant, belonging to them, asked me, where they should march? I shewed him the party he was to fight; and he, like a true bred Englishman, marched, and I caused the soldiers to follow him; which presently fell upon the enemy, and losing that wing the whole army gave ground and fled. Such valiant acts were done by contemptible instruments: The major had been called to a council of war, but that he cried *peccavi*.

These Lancashire troops, under the command of "Colonel-General" Ashton, appear to have been brave fellows enough; but, like militiamen in general, they appear to have had only lax notions of discipline. If not actually mutinous, they sometimes lacked the subordination essential to military discipline. Their qualities Captain Hodgson sums up in the following pithy sentences—

The Lancashire foot were as stout men as were in the world, and as brave firemen. I have often told them, they were as good fighters, and as great plunderers, as ever went to a field.

6. He had overcome a cavalry officer, and "appropriated" his horse.

CHAPTER 4

Athelstan's Great Victory at Brunanburh, A.D. 937

Harold—(On the morn of the battle of Senlac or Hastings)—Our
guardsmen have slept well since we came in?
Leofwin.— . . . . They are up again
And chanting that old song of Brunanburg,
Where England conquer'd.
Tennyson's Harold.

Upwards of three centuries had elapsed since the departure of the Roman legions from Britain, and the presumedly first regularly organised invasion of the island by the Angles, Saxons, and Jutes, when a new enemy of the same Teutonic blood and language appeared upon her shores. The country had been but partially conquered by the first Teutonic invaders. Picts and Scots held their own in Ireland and that portion of Great Britain to the north of the estuaries of the Clyde and the Forth. The Britons were not only masters in old Cornwall and in a more extended territory than is now included in the present principality of Wales, but they remained dominant in Strathclyde and Cumberland, which comprised the lands on the western side of the island between the Clyde estuary and Morecambe Bay. Christianity had become the recognised religious faith of both the Britons and the Teutons, but the newly arrived kinsmen of the latter were still worshippers of Odin, and marched to battle with his sacred "totem" or cognizance, the "swart raven" emblazoned on their banners. The *Anglo-Saxon Chronicle*, under the date 787, says—

This year king Bertric took to wife Eadburga, King Offa's daughter; and in his days first came three ships of Northmen,

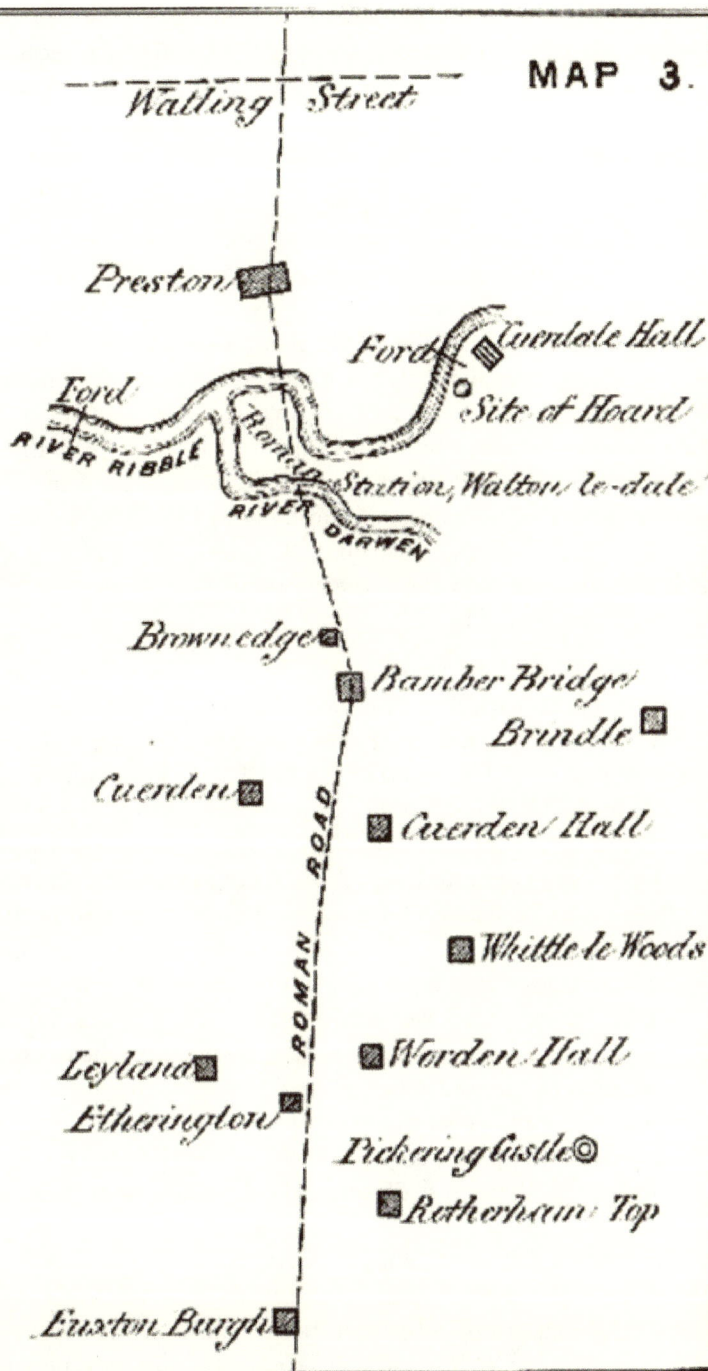

MAP 3.

Watling Street

Preston

Ford

Ford

RIVER RIBBLE

Roman Ford

Ford

Cuerdale Hall

Site of Hoard

Station, Walton le-dale

RIVER DARWEN

Brownedge

Bamber Bridge

Brindle

Cuerden

ROAD

Cuerden Hall

Whittle le Woods

ROMAN

Worden Hall

Leyland

Etherington

Pickering Castle

Rotherham Top

Euxton Burgh

out of Hœretha-land (Denmark.) And then the reve rode to the place, and would have driven them to the king's town, because he knew not who they were: and they there slew him. These were the first ships of Danish men which sought the land of the English nation.

These three ships landed in Dorsetshire, and the *gerefa* or *reve*, named Beaduheard, of Dorchester, supposed them to be contraband traders rather than pirates. This mistake cost him his life, as well as the lives of the whole of his retinue.

The conflicts which followed for many years afterwards between these heathen pirates and their Christianised kinsmen were characterised by deeds of remorseless atrocity as well as of indomitable valour. Truly, every now relatively civilized nation has had to pass through what may not be inaptly termed its Bashi-Bazouk stage of culture before from it evolved its present more highly developed intellectual and moral human features. Mr. Jno. R. Green (*Short History of the English People*,) sums up the more prominent characteristics of this internecine strife as follows:—

> The first sight of the Danes is as if the hand of the dial of history had gone back three hundred years. The same Norwegian fiords, the same Frisian sandbanks, pour forth their pirate fleets as in the days of Hengest and Cerdic. There is the same wild panic as the black boats of the invaders strike inland along the river reaches, or moor round the river islets, the same sights of horror—firing of homesteads, slaughter of men, women driven off to slavery or shame, children tossed on pikes or sold in the market-place—as when the English invaders attacked Britain. Christian priests were again slain at the altar by worshippers of Woden, for the Danes were still heathen. Letters, arts, religion, governments disappeared before these Northmen as before the Northmen of old. But when the wild burst of the storm was over, land, people, government reappeared unchanged. England still remained England; the Danes sank quietly into the mass of those around them; and Woden yielded without a struggle to Christ.
>
> The secret of this difference between the two invasions was that the battle was no longer between men of different races. It was no longer a fight between Briton and German, between Englishmen and Welshmen. The Danes were the same people

130

in blood and speech with the people they attacked; and were in fact Englishmen bringing back to an England that had forgotten its origins the barbaric England of its pirate forefathers. Nowhere over Europe was the fight so fierce, because nowhere else were the combatants men of one blood and one speech. But just for this reason the fusion of the Northmen with their foes was nowhere so peaceful and complete.

The chief Danish ravages for nearly a century were confined to the southern coast and the coast of East Anglia. In 855, the *Chronicle* says—

The heathen men for the first time remained over winter in Sheppey.

In 867, it records that:

This year the Danish army went from East Anglia over the mouth of the Humber to York, in North-humbria. And there was much dissention among that people, and they had cast out their king Osbert, and had taken to themselves a king, Ælla, not of royal blood; but late in the year they resolved that they would fight against the army, and therefore they gathered a large force, and fought the army at the town of York, and stormed the town, and some of them got within and there was an excessive slaughter made of the North-humbrians, some within, some without, and the kings were both slain, and the remainder made peace with the army.

Some writers say that Ælla was put to death with the most frightful tortures in revenge for similar cruel treatment, on his part, of his conquered foe, Ragnar Lodbrock, by the three sons of that somewhat mythical hero, named Halfden, Ingwar, and Hubba, who commanded the expedition. The story runs that Ragnar, being taken prisoner by Ælla, was thrown into a dungeon, and bitten to death by vipers. This Ragnar, however, has proved so troublesome to northern scholars, that many regard him as a mythical personage, belonging to an earlier, or what they term the "heroic period." Scandinavian reliable *history* only dates from about the middle of the ninth century. Ælla usurped the Northumbrian throne in the year 862, and Mr. J. A. Blackwell, in his edition of Mallett's *Northern Antiquities*, says:

"Ragnar's death is placed by Suhm, who has brought it down

to the latest possible epoch, in 794, and by other writers at a much earlier period.

Some of the deeds attributed to this hero are unquestionably mythical. From the "Death Song," said to have been written by him, but which Mr. Blackwell regards as more probably the composition of a Skald of the ninth century, we learn that Ragnar succeeded, like Indra, Perseus, St. George, and other solar heroes, in conquering a monster serpent that held in captivity Thora, the daughter of a chieftain of Gothland, and received the lady in marriage, as the reward of his prowess. In order to protect himself against the serpent's venom, it is said that Ragnar "put on shaggy trousers, from which circumstance he was afterwards called Lodbrok (*Shaggy-brogues*)." Be this as it may, Ingwar, his presumed son, on the defeat of Ælla and Osbert, ascended the Northumbrian throne, and the Danes remained masters of the situation, until the partition of the kingdom between Godrun and Alfred the Great gave them peaceful possession of the territory.

In the year 876, Halfden, a famous Danish Viking, according to the *Anglo-Saxon Chronicle*, "appropriated the lands of Northumbria; and they thenceforth continued ploughing and tilling them." Consequently, from this period, the great mass of the men of Scandinavian blood in Northumbria must be regarded rather in the light of emigrants or settlers than roving pirates, although, doubtless, with them the sword was always ready to supersede the ploughshare whenever the arrival of a fleet of their buccaneering relatives on the coast afforded an opportunity for a successful foray on the lands of their Anglo-Saxon neighbours.

On the death of Edward the Elder, in the year 925, the "right royal" grandson of the Great Alfred, the "golden haired" Athelstan, succeeded to the kingdom of Wessex and its dependencies, which included the whole of England south of the Humber and the Mersey, with the exception of Cornwall and East Anglia, and the "overlordship" of the whole of the Anglo-Saxon and Danish rulers, as well as those of the Welsh and Scots, whose kings rendered him homage and acknowledged him the legitimate successor to his father Edward, whom they regarded as "their Father, Lord, and Protector." Edward the Elder was, at the time of his highest prosperity, unquestionably the most powerful "*Bretwalda*" or "overlord" that had ruled in Britain since the departure of the Romans.

Soon after Athelstan's succession, however, the kings of the present

Principality, or North Wales, as the whole country from the Severn to the Dee was then called, rebelled against the authority of the hated fair-haired Sassenach. Athelstan instantly attacked Edwall Voel, king of Gwynnedd, and wrested the entire sovereignty of his dominion from him. He, however, on the submission of the other Welsh princes, and their performance of homage to him at his court held at Hereford, generously restored it to him. Afterwards the country between the Severn and the Wye were added to Mercia, and a heavy tribute was imposed on all the revolted Welsh monarchs. Twenty pounds weight of gold and three hundred pounds of silver were to be yearly paid into the treasury, or, as it was then styled, the "Hoard" of the "King of London." To this was to be added an annual gift of twenty thousand beeves and the swiftest hounds and hawks that the country possessed.

The Cornish Britons, or West Welsh, as they were then termed, were afterwards subdued, and thus all Britain south of the Humber and the Mersey again acknowledged Athelstan's supremacy or "over-lordship."

In the year 925, the Anglo-Saxon Chronicle informs us that Athelstan and Sihtric (or Sigtryg), king of the North-humbrians, "came together at Tamworth, on the 3rd before the *Kalends* of February; and Athelstan gave him his sister." But this marriage failed to secure the proposed future alliance between the Scandinavian and Anglo-Saxon sovereigns. The Dane, who had embraced Christianity, relapsed into the faith of his forefathers and returned his wife to her former home. Sihtric's death, however, intervened between the repudiation of Queen Editha, who afterwards became Abbess of Tamworth, and the vengeance of Athelstan, which fell upon Anlaf and Godefrid, sons of Sihtric by a former marriage. Anlaf fled to Ireland, on the east coast of which the Danes held the supreme authority, and his brother sought refuge with Constantine, king of the Scots. Referring to these events the *Anglo-Saxon Chronicle* says—

> *A. 926.* This year fiery lights appeared in the north part of the heavens. And Sihtric perished; and king Athelstan obtained the kingdom of the North-humbrians. And he ruled all the kings who were in the island; first, Howel, king of the West-Welsh; and Constantine, king of the Scots; and Owen, king of the Monmouth people; and Aldred, son of Ealdulf, of Bambrough: and they confirmed the peace by pledge, and by oaths, at the place which is called Eamot, on the 4th before the *Ides* of July;

and they renounced all idolatry, and after that submitted to him in peace.

But the peace was not of very long duration, for the king of the Scots raised the standard of revolt, and the old chronicler, or perhaps a successor, tells us that in the year 933, "Athelstan went into Scotland, as well with a land army as with a fleet, and ravaged a great part of it." This defeat of the Scottish king for a time restored Athelstan's dominion, but the peace which followed was, four years afterwards, broken by a powerful combination of Athelstan's enemies, which shook the "overlordship" of the English monarch to its foundation, and threatened the safety of his inherited kingdoms. The Scots, the Cumbrian Britons, the North and West Welsh, entered into a league with Anlaf of Dublin and the Danish chiefs of Northumbria and their Scandinavian allies to lower the prestige of the English monarch, and to seat the son of Sihtric on the throne of his ancestors. This fierce conflict culminated in the great battle of Brunanburh, in the year 937, in which, after a desperate two days' struggle, the confederate forces of his enemies were utterly routed, and Athelstan reigned supreme monarch to the end of his kingly career.

There is some difficulty in determining the exact date of this celebrated engagement. Sharon-Turner gives it as 934. Worsaae in his *Danes and Norwegians in England*, says 937. Ethelwerd's *Chronicle* says 939. Sharon-Turner refers to the fact that one MS. of the *Anglo-Saxon Chronicle* gives the date 937, notwithstanding which he prefers 934. Dr. Freeman in his *Old English History* adheres to 937, which seems to be the most probable date.

We find that British Christians, as on previous occasions, espoused the cause of the heathen Danes, rather than fraternize with their hated Anglo-Saxon rivals, the disciples of Augustine and Paulinus. Thus many elements combined to render this battle one of the bloodiest and most destructive ever fought on British soil. The great struggle did not take place immediately on the arrival of Anlaf and his allies. Athelstan's two governors, Gudrekir and Alfgeirr first confronted the invaders. The former was slain and the latter fled to his sovereign, with the news of their discomfiture. Athelstan, with wise forethought, tried the effect of diplomacy, if only for the purpose of gaining sufficient time for the assembling of all his forces before staking his sovereignty upon the issue of a single battle.

The authorities, contemporary or nearly so, for the details of this decisive campaign, although meagre in comparison with those of more recent struggles, are nevertheless fuller than usual for the period. We have the poem in the *Anglo-Saxon Chronicle*, a notice in Ethelwerd's *Chronicle*, and some Scandinavian accounts, notably Egil's Saga. Sharon-Turner, however, regards the northern authorities as not entitled to implicit reliance, as their great object was the laudation of Egil and Thorolf, Scandinavian mercenaries in the pay of Athelstan, who, they contend, mainly contributed to the victory by the annihilation of the "disorderly Irish" contingent.

Athelstan, when his diplomatic *finesse* had answered his purpose, suddenly appeared at Brunanburh, and pitched his camp in front of the enemy. It is related that Anlaf, taken by surprise, imitated Alfred's stratagem, and entered the royal camp in the disguise of a harper. He was admitted into the presence of Athelstan, who was ever liberal in his patronage of poets and musicians, and the Danish king played, sang, and danced before the assembled chieftains, at a banquet, in the enjoyment of which he found them engaged previously to the holding of a council of war. On his dismissal a purse, filled with silver groats, was given to him as a reward for his services. Anlaf's observant military eye had detected the weakest point in his adversary's position, and the exact locality in which the royal tent was pitched, and he determined to surprise the camp by a sudden night attack, and either slay or carry off the king a prisoner.

One false step, however, robbed him of the advantage his daring had gained. On leaving the enemy's lines, he was observed by a sentinel, who had formerly served under him, to bury the king's gratuity, which he disdained to appropriate to other use, in a hole in the earth. This aroused the soldier's suspicion, and Athelstan was informed of the circumstance. The king, in the first instance, was disposed to treat the man somewhat harshly, and demanded why the information as to the identity of the pretended itinerant minstrel had not been communicated to him before his departure. To this the faithful soldier replied:

> Nay, by the same oath of fealty which binds me to thee, O king, was I once bound to Anlaf; and had I betrayed him, with equal justice mightest thou have expected treachery from me. But hear my counsel. Whilst awaiting further reinforcements, take away thy tent from the spot upon which it now stands, and thus mayest thou ward off the blow of thine enemy.

This advice Athelstan followed, and shortly afterwards the Bishop of Sherborne arrived with his contingent, and pitched his tent in the locality vacated by his royal master, which circumstance cost him his life during the night surprise which followed. We have Alfred's harper story on the authority of Ingulf and William of Malmesbury, the former of whom was born in 1030, and the latter in 1095 or 1096, so that they were recording events which had transpired between one and two centuries before their own adult experience.

The Anlaf tale is too exact a counterpart of the one related about Alfred, not to suggest doubt as to its veracity; or, if it be a veritable incident in the life of the Scandinavian warrior, the doubt will have to be transferred to the story related of his Saxon predecessor. It is not very probable so transparent an artifice would succeed a second time, especially when played upon such a clear-headed chieftain as Alfred's grandson.[1] But, however Anlaf gained his information, the night the attack took place, Adils, a Welsh prince, detected the strategy of Athelstan.

After the death of the Bishop of Sherborne, he and Hyngr (a chieftain described in Egil's Saga as a Welshman, but whose name, Sharon-Turner thinks, sounds very like a Danish one), led the attack on the main body of the English army. But Athelstan was prepared, and Thorolf and Alfgeirr's detachments were instantly opposed to them. Alfgeirr was soon overpowered and fled, on perceiving which Thorolf threw his shield behind him, and hewed his way with his heavy two-hand sword through the opposing mass until he reached the standard of Hyngr. A few moments decided the fate of that chieftain. Thorolf ordered Egil, though weakened by the defeat and flight of Alfgeirr, to resist Adils, but to be prepared to retreat to the cover of a neighbouring wood, if necessary. Adils, mourning the death of his colleague, at length gave way, and the preliminary nocturnal combat ended.

After a day's rest,[2] Egil led the van of the Anglo-Saxon army, and

---

1. Mr. F. Metcalfe, in his *Englishman and Scandinavian*, says,—"It is this same historian (William of Malmesbury), and not Asser, who relates the story of Alfred masquerading as a minstrel, and so gaining free access to the Danish camp, meanwhile learning their plans. It is not mentioned in the most ancient Saxon accounts. Indeed, it sounds more like a Scandinavian than a Saxon story, an echo of which has reached us in the tale of King Estmere, who adopted a similar disguise. A story was current of Olaf Cuaran entering Athelstan's camp disguised as a harper two days before the Battle of Brunanburh."

2. Some writers say two days intervened, and Sir Francis Palgrave says the main battle was but a continuation of the night attack, and was therefore fought on the following day.

Thorolf opposed the "irregular Irish," which formed part of Anlaf's own division, and extended to the wood previously mentioned. Turketal, the English chancellor, a man of stalwart proportions, who commanded the citizens of London, and Singin of Worcestershire, were opposed to Constantine, king of the Scots, while Athelstan, at the head of his West Saxons, confronted Anlaf in person. Thorolf attempted to turn the enemies' flank, when Adils rushed from his ambush in the wood, and countered the movement.

Egils saw with dismay Thorolf's banner retreating. He knew by this that he must have fallen; and, rushing to the spot, he rallied the scattered band, successfully renewed the attack, and, in Sharon-Turner's words, "sacrificed Adils to the manes of Thorolf." The councillor pierced the enemy's centre, heedless of the arrows and spears which fastened on his armour. Constantine and he met and fought hand to hand for some time, and Singer slew the prince, his son, who fought valiantly by his father's side.

This vigorous and successful onslaught produced a panic among the Scots, and correspondingly elated the English. In the meanwhile Athelstan and his brother, Edmund, the Atheling, were engaged with the main body of the enemy under Anlaf. The grandson of the Great Alfred and the presumed grandson of Radnor Lodbrog contended both for dominion and renown. In the midst of the fight Athelstan's sword-blade snapped near the handle. Another was supplied to him, it was said, by miraculous agency, which saved his life. At length the tremendous struggle, which lasted throughout the day, was brought to a close by Turketal chasing the Scots from the battlefield, and turning Anlaf's flank.

Immense slaughter ensued; the enemy's ranks began rapidly to thin; the English shouted "victory!" and Athelstan, profiting by the auspicious opportunity, ordered his banner to the front, and by a determined and well-directed onslaught, broke the enemy's now enfeebled ranks. They fled in various directions, and, according to Egil's saga, "the plain was filled with their bodies." Anlaf and his immediate followers narrowly escaped to their ships and embarked for Ireland. Sharon-Turner says—

> Thus terminated this dangerous and important conflict. Its successful issue was of such consequence, that it raised Athelstan in the eyes of all Europe. The kings of the continent sought his friendship, and England began to assume a majestic port

amid the other nations of the west. Amongst the Anglo-Saxons it excited such rejoicings that not only their poets aspired to commemorate it, but the songs were so popular, that one of them is inserted in the *Saxon Chronicle* as the best memorial of the event.

The following is Dr. Giles's literal rendering of this remarkable poem into modern English:—

A. 937.—Here Athelstan, king,
of earls the lord,
of heroes the bracelet giver,
and his brother eke,
Edmund etheling,
life-long glory
in battle won
with edges of swords
near Brunanburh.
The board-walls they clove,
they hewed the war-lindens,
Hamora lafan'
offspring of Edward,
such was their noble nature
from their ancestors,
that they in battle oft
'gainst every foe
the land defended,
hoards and homes.
The foe they crushed,
the Scottish people
and the shipmen
fated fell.
The field 'dæniede'
with warriors' blood,
since the sun up
at morning tide—
mighty planet—
glided o'er grounds,
God's candle bright,
the eternal Lord's—
till the noble creature

sank to her settle.
There lay many a warrior
by javelins strewed;
northern men
over shield shot;
so the Scots, eke,
weary, war-sad.
West Saxons onwards
throughout the day,
in bands,
pursued the footsteps
of the loathed nations.
They hewed the fugitives
behind, amain,
with swords mill-sharp.
Mercians refused not
the hard hand-play
to any heroes
who, with Anlaf,
over the ocean,
in the ship's bosom,
this land sought
fated to the fight.
Five lay
on the battle-stead,
youthful kings,
by swords in slumber laid:
so seven, eke,
of Anlaf's earls;
of the army countless,
shipmen and Scots.
There was made flee
the North-men's chieftain,
by need constrained,
to the ship's prow
with a little band.
The bark drove afloat;
the king departed,
on the fallow flood
his life preserved.

So there, eke, the sage
came by flight
to his country north,
Constantine,
hoary warrior.
He had no cause to exult
in the communion of swords.
Here was his kindred band
of friends o'erthrown
on the folk-stead,
in battle slain;
and his son he left
on the slaughter-place
mangled with wounds,
young in the fight.
He had no cause to boast,
hero grizzly haired,
of the bill-clashing,
the old deceiver;
nor Anlaf the moor,
with the remnant of their armies;
they had no cause to laugh
that they in war's works
the better men were
in the battle-stead,
at the conflict of banners,
meeting of spears,
concourse of men,
traffic of weapons,
that they on the slaughter-field
with Edward's
offspring played.
The North-men departed
in their nailed barks—
bloody relic of darts—
on roaring ocean,
o'er the deep water,
Dublin to seek;
again Ireland
shamed in mind.

So, too, the brothers,
both together,
king and etheling,
their country sought,
West-Saxons' land,
in the war exulting.
They left behind them,
the corse to devour,
the sallowy kite
and the swarthy raven
with horned nib,
and the dusky 'pada,'
erne white-tailed,
the corse to enjoy,—
greedy war-hawk,
and the grey beast,
wolf of the wood.
Carnage greater has not been
in this island
ever yet
of people slain,
before this,
by edges of swords,
as the books say—
old writers—
since from the east hither
Angles and Saxons
came to land,—
o'er the broad seas
Britain sought,—
mighty war-smiths
the Welsh o'ercame;
earls most bold
this earth obtained.

Some of the MSS. of the *Chronicle* have the following additional reference to the battle:—

A. 937. This year King Athelstan and Edmund his brother led a force to Brunanburh, and there fought against Anlaf; and Christ helping, had the victory; and they there slew five kings and

141

seven earls.

Simeon, of Durham, says one of these five monarchs was "Eligenius, an under-king of Deira," or the eastern portion of the then kingdom of Northumbria.

Athelstan died in 940, and, in the following year, the *Chronicle* says his successor "Edmund received king Anlaf at baptism."

In 942, it says—"This year King Anlaf died." There were, however, two other chieftains of the same name, who flourished somewhat later.

Historians are scarcely, even at the present day, unanimous in their views as to what monarch ought to be regarded as the first "king of England." Some say Egbert; but his authority rarely if ever extended over the whole of the country now so named, and a very large proportion of it was merely a kind of nominal "over lordship," which carried with it very little governing influence, and, such as it was, it was held on a very precarious tenure. Others contend that the distinction belongs to Alfred the Great. Yet Alfred, though beloved by all the English-speaking people in the land, was compelled to share the territory with his Danish rival, Gothrun. Sharon-Turner says—

> The truth seems to be that Alfred was the first monarch of the *Anglo-Saxons*, but Athelstan was the first monarch of *England*.
>
> After the Battle of Brunanburh, Athelstan had no competitor; he was the *immediate Sovereign of all England*. He was even *nominal* lord of Wales and Scotland.

This seems to be the true solution of the query.

It is a most remarkable circumstance that the site of this great victory, notwithstanding the magnitude of the contending armies and the importance of its political and social results, was, until recently, at least, absolutely unknown, and it cannot yet be said that the true locality has been demonstrated with sufficient clearness to entirely remove all doubt. Many places have been suggested on the most frivolous grounds. The question where is, or was, Brunanburh is still sounding in the ear of the historical student, and echo merely answers "Where?" Yet I think I have made the nearest approach to the solution of this problem, in the *History of Preston and its Environs*, that has yet been attempted, and further investigation enables me to add considerably to the evidence there adduced.

It is, perhaps, necessary that some attempt should be made to determine the cause or causes why the site of so important a victory, celebrated in the finest extant short poem in the Anglo-Saxon tongue, and so important in its political results, should have become lost both to the history and tradition of the English victors. At first sight there appears something singularly exceptionable in the fact. But a closer inspection of the details of what may be termed the Anglo-Saxon period of conflict with their Scandinavian enemies, Danish, Norwegian, or Norman-French, soon removes this impression, the sites of many other, almost equally important struggles, and notoriously some of those in which the Great Alfred was engaged, having been subjected to similar doubt, if not oblivion.

In the first place it must not be forgotten that after the death of Athelstan, the Danish invasions were renewed, and, after various successes and defeats, the Scandinavian monarchs, Sweyn and Canute, before the end of the tenth century, ruled despotically over all England. Even the temporary restoration of the Anglo-Saxon dynastic element, in the person of Edward the Confessor, in consequence of his Norman-French connection and early education, did little to remove the pressure of the foreign yoke, in the provinces at least; and what influence it may have exerted was speedily eradicated by the decisive victory of William the Norman, near Hastings, in the middle of the following century.

Conquest, in those days, meant subjugation to the extent of a deprivation of all rights—at least all political rights—and many social privileges, and absolute serfdom for the great mass of the population. Consequently it was the policy of the conquerors to ignore, and, as far as possible, enforce the ignorement of all past glorious achievements of the ancestors of the subjugated peoples. Doubtless, tradition would still, with its tenacious grasp, retain some recollection of the great exploits of their forefathers, and, in secret, the people would cherish their memory with a more intense love, on account of the persecution to which its open expression would be subjected. But in those days there were no printing presses, nor journalism, local or metropolitan. The people could not read, and even the nobles, in the main, like old King Cole, in the song, because he could afford to salary a secretary, "scorned the fetters of the four and twenty letters, and it saved them a vast deal of trouble."

Now, these secretaries were almost, if not entirely, ecclesiastics; and they were likewise the only literary, or learned men, existing during the period to which I refer. These ecclesiastics, in different monasteries, kept records of the general events of the period in which they lived, of a very meagre character, and devoted more time and space to matters ecclesiastical, as might reasonably be anticipated. Again, when the Danish and Norman warriors obtained the supreme power, it is easy to understand that the ecclesiastical domination was speedily transferred to their clerical *confreres*; and, of course, whatever obscurity rested on the details of previous victories or glories of the subject race, would be intensified rather than lessened, by any action of theirs, even supposing (which is anything but probable), that they themselves possessed much authentic information respecting such events.

Subsequent writers, of course, dealt largely in mere conjecture, on the flimsiest of evidence; and, as they sometimes differ so widely from each other, or as they are so obscure in their topographical definitions and nomenclature, little is derivable from their labours of value to the modern historian and antiquary. Consequently, although there are many references to the great battle itself, both in the several chronicles, the poem to which I have referred, and in some Scandinavian sagas, written in honour of two of their warriors of the free-lance, or Dugal Dalgetty class, who fought on the side of the English monarch, the site of the great conflict has remained doubtful to the present time.

Henry of Huntingdon, who wrote in the earlier portion of the twelfth century, referring to the twelve presumed victories of Arthur, accounts for the then loss of their sites in the following characteristic fashion—

These battles and battlefields are described by Gildas, (*Nennius*,) the historian, but in our times the places are unknown, the Providence of God, we consider, having so ordered it that popular applause and flattery, and transitory glory, might be of no account.

The clerical historian seems to have thoroughly understood the motives of his predecessors in the destruction of the records of a heretical or pagan race.

Mr. Daniel H. Haigh, in his *Conquest of Britain by the Saxons*, referring to the absence of Runic inscriptions in the south of England, and their partial preservation in the Northumbrian kingdom, has the following pertinent observations:—

The first missionaries, St. Augustine and his brethren, used all their endeavours to destroy every monument of Runic antiquity, because runes had been the means of pagan augury, and of preserving the memory of pagan hymns and incantations; for, knowing how prone the common people were to their ancient superstitions (of which even after the lapse of twelve centuries many vestiges still remain), and how difficult it would be to teach them to distinguish the use of a thing from its abuse, they feared that their labours would be in vain so long as the monuments of ancient superstition remained.

So every Runic writing disappeared; and we may well believe, that records which to us would be invaluable, perished in the general destruction. In the first instance S. Gregory had commanded that everything connected with paganism should be destroyed; but afterwards, in a letter to S. Milletus, he recommended that the symbols only of paganism should be done away with, but that the sanctuaries should be consecrated and used as churches. These instructions were in force when S. Paulinus evangelized Northumbria; and we cannot doubt that the work of destruction would be effectively done under the auspices of a prince whose police was so vigorous as we are informed that Eadwine's was. But after his death, and the flight of S. Paulinus, the restoration of Christianity in Northumbria was effected by missionaries of the Irish school, whose fathers in Ireland had pursued from the first a different policy, by allowing the memorials of antiquity to remain, and contenting themselves with consecrating the monuments of paganism, and marking them with the symbols of Christianity.

Under their auspices Runic writing was permitted, for we can trace its use in Northumbria to the very times of S. Oswald, whilst every vestige has disappeared of the Runic records of an earlier period. Mercia received its Christianity from the Irish school of Lindisfarne, and we have runes on the coins of the first Christian kings, Peada andŒthelræd.

But for the zealous labour of Archbishop Parker, in the sixteenth century, even few of the remaining Anglo-Saxon MSS. would have been preserved to the present day. John Bale, writing in 1549, says—

A great number of them that purchased the monasteries reserved the books of those libraries; some to scour their candlesticks, some to rub their boots, some they sold to grocers and soapsellers, some they sent over sea to the book-binders, not in small numbers, but at times whole ships full, to the wondering of foreign nations.

Religious and political rancour has too often consigned to destruction the archives and monuments of hated rivals. Cardinal Ximines, somewhat earlier, committed to the flames an immense mass of valuable Arabic MSS. and, not long afterwards, Archbishop Zumarraga committed a similar act of insensate vandalism on the picture-written national archives of Mexico. Our medieval historians, indeed, have themselves much to answer for in this direction. Strype says that Polydore Vergil, having, by licence from Henry VIII., when writing his history, procured many valuable books from various libraries in England, on its conclusion, piled "those same books together, and set them all on a light fire."

Mr. Frederick Metcalf (*Englishman and Scandinavian*) waxed wrath as he contemplated the irreparable loss sustained through the ignorance and fanaticism of our forefathers. He exclaims—

> Cart loads of Old English mythical and heroic epics, finished histories in the vernacular, heaps of pieces teeming with sprightly humour, with vivid portraiture, with precious touches of nature, may or may not have been destroyed by the Danes, by the Normans, in their contempt for everything Anglo-Saxon, by insensate scribes in want of vellum—who scraped out things of beauty to make room for their own doting effusions, or pasted the leaves of MSS. together to make bindings—by the Reformers, by the Roundheads, by fire, by crass folly.

Independently of wilful neglect or active destruction, the Anglo-Norman transcripts of previous Anglo-Saxon MSS. now existing are not only rarities, but wretchedly deficient, owing to both accidental damage, and the carelessness, or ignorance, of their monkish transcribers. Thorpe, referring to the only existing early MS. of the poem *Beowulf*, in his preface to his work on the *Anglo-Saxon Poems of Beowulf, the Scôp or Gleeman's Tale, and the Fight at Finnesburg*, says—

> Unfortunately, as of Cædmon and the Codex Exoniensis, there is only a single manuscript of Beowulf extant, which I take to be of the first half of the eleventh century (MS. *Cott. Vitellius* A. 15). All manuscripts of Anglo-Saxon poetry are deplorably inaccurate, evincing, in almost every page, the ignorance of an illiterate scribe, frequently (as was the monastic custom) copying from dictation; but of all Anglo-Saxon manuscripts,

that of Beowulf may, I believe, be conscientiously pronounced the worst, independently of its present lamentable condition, in consequence of the fire at Cotton House, in 1731, whereby it was seriously injured, being partially rendered as friable as touchwood. In perfect accordance with this judgment of the manuscript and its writer is the testimony of Dr. Grundtvig, who says—'The ancient scribe did not rightly understand what he himself was writing; and, what was worse, the conflagration in 1731 had rendered a part wholly or almost illegible.' Mr. Kemble's words are to the same effect—'The manuscript of Beowulf is unhappily among the most corrupt of all the Anglo-Saxon manuscripts, and corrupt they all are without exception.'

My attention was first called to the probable site of Athelstan's great victory at Brunanburh, when dealing with the "great Cuerdale Find," of May, 1840. Mr. Hawkins, vice-president of the Numismatic Society, who devoted much attention to the contents of this remarkable chest, says "the hoard consisted of about 975 ounces of silver in ingots, ornaments, etc., besides about 7,000 coins of various descriptions." From my own knowledge many of the coins and some of the ornaments were never seen by Mr. Hawkins. Referring to this subject, in the *History of Preston,* I say—

Many of the coins unquestionably found their way surreptitiously into the hands of collectors; consequently there is some difficulty in determining the precise number discovered. It is pretty generally believed, however, that the chest originally contained about ten thousand coins. (These coins were all of silver). Many of the silver rings and smaller bars were, likewise, 'appropriated' before any record of the 'find' was made.

The collection contained numismatic treasures both of English and foreign mintage, and all were coined antecedent to the great battle, although the most modern amongst them date within a very few years of that event. Dr. Worsaae, the celebrated Danish antiquary, speaking of this "find," says—

To judge from the coins, which, with few exceptions, were minted between the years 815 and 930, the treasure must have been buried in the first half of the tenth century, or about a hundred years before the time of Canute the Great.

My position, therefore, is that this great treasure chest was buried near the "pass of the Ribble," at Cuerdale, opposite Preston, during this troubled period, and probably on the retreat of the confederated Irish, Scotch, Welsh, Scandinavian, and Anglo-Danish armies, after their disastrous defeat by the English under Athelstan, at the great battle of Brunanburh, in 937, which may not inaptly be styled, on account of its magnitude and important results, the Waterloo of the tenth century.

Various places have from time to time been suggested as the probable locality of the conflict, but upon the very slenderest of evidence. Some say Colecroft, near Axminster, Devonshire. One authority assigns the following reason for this site—

> Axminster is *supposed* to have derived its present name from a college of priests, founded here by Athelstan, to pray for the souls of those who fell in the conflict, and who were buried in the cemetery of Axminster; there were five kings and eight earls amongst them.

A claim has been advanced for Beverley in Yorkshire, for a similar reason. But the founding of a monastery, or other expression of thanksgiving for a victory, does not necessarily indicate the locality of the conflict. William the Conqueror did certainly found Battle Abbey on the site of his great victory; but such a practice is by no means of ordinary occurrence, and without corroborative evidence is valueless. Camden thought the battle was fought at Ford, near Bromeridge, in Northumberland. Skene, in his *Celtic Scotland*, prefers Aldborough, on the Ouse, and regards the huge monoliths, known as "the devil's arrows," as memorials of the victory. Gibson and others suggest Bromborough, in Cheshire.

The editor of the *Imperial Gazetteer* assigns Broomridge, no doubt on Camden's authority, and Brinkburn, in the Rothsay district, in Northumberland, or some other, as probable sites of the battle. Brinkburn is said to be the "true situation of Brunanburh," in *Beauties of England and Wales*. The name was written in 1154, by John of Hexham, Brincaburgh. Banbury, in Oxfordshire, and Bourne, and the neighbourhood of Barton-on-Humber, in Lincolnshire, and a Bambro', a Bambury, and some other places have likewise found advocates.

Dr. Giles, in his annotation of Ethelwerd's *Chronicle*, fixes Brunanburh at Brumby, in Lincolnshire, but he assigns no reasons for his preference. Brunton, in Northumberland, and, I believe, some other places, have been suggested. The mere identity of the name Brunanburh, in some corrupted form, though important, is insufficient, without corroborative evidence, simply because the names of so many places, in various parts of the country, admit of such derivation. There are several even in Lancashire, to which I shall afterwards call attention. Localities on the east, the south, and the west coasts of England have each found advocates, some, certainly, on very slight grounds.

Mr. Weddle, of Wargrove, near Warrington, in his essay on the site, in 1857, pertinently reminds the investigator that the very "uncertainty of the whereabouts of the battlefield" is a good reason why it should be sought for "in some place half-forgotten." Such being the case, I may, without much presumption, after studying the subject now for five and twenty years, adhere to my previously suggested solution of this great historical and topographical enigma.

The available evidence is very diversified in its character, and may be dealt with under several distinct heads. In the first place I will endeavour to show why I maintain that the discovery of the long buried treasure at Cuerdale, in 1840, has furnished the key by which we may probably unlock the mystery.

From its great value in the tenth century, the evidence of recent mintage at the time of its deposition, and the vast number of rare and foreign coins, many of which were struck by Scandinavian kings or jarls, all lead to the conjecture that the treasure had not originally belonged to some private individual or inferior chieftain. It must not be forgotten that coin was first made "sterling" in the year 1216, before which time Stowe says rents were mostly paid in "kind," and money was found only in the coffers of the barons.

The great probability, therefore, appears to be that some powerful monarch, or confederacy, owned the chest, and that its burial near one of the three fords at the "pass of the Ribble" was caused by some signal discomfiture or military defeat, in order to prevent its falling into the hands of the enemy. Its non-recovery afterwards would naturally result from the slaughter of the parties acquainted with the precise locality of its deposit in the disastrous riot attendant upon so great victory as that achieved by Athelstan at Brunanburh. Tradition had, however, preserved the memory of its burial, but the exact site was unknown.

It was popularly thought, however, that it could be seen from the hill on which the church of Walton-le-dale stands, and which overlooks all the three fords which constituted the "famous pass of the Ribble." The late Mr. Barton F. Allen, of Preston, remembered that in his youth a farmer ploughed a field which had remained in pasture from time immemorial, in hope of finding the treasure. At the time I came upon the Roman remains, near the great central ford, 1855, I was surprised to learn a rumour was abroad that we had "come on't goud" at last. This resulted from the fact that the Anglo-Danish hoard consisted entirely of silver, and the belief of the workmen that the Roman brass coins, found at the time, from their colour, when polished, were golden ones.

I therefore contend that these facts (taken in conjunction with the more important one, that the date of the deposit, as demonstrated by the coins themselves, coincides with that of Athelstan's great victory), indicate, in a very high degree, the probable connection of the two events. The burial of treasure, in times of great disaster, was a very ordinary occurrence during the Roman dominion in Britain, and was not unusual with their successors, the Anglo-Saxons and Danes. Two hoards, one found at Walmersley, to the north of Bury, and the other at Whittle, near the present presumed site of Athelstan's victory, to the south of the Ribble, from the date of the coins, coincide with the time of the defeat of the usurpers Carausius and Allectus, commanders of the Roman fleet stationed to protect the shores of Britain from the ravages of Saxon pirates. Later the Anglo-Saxon Chronicle says—

A. 418, this year the Romans collected all the treasures that were in Britain, and some they hid in the earth, so that no one has since been able to find them; and some they carried with them into Gaul.

Ethelwerd's *Chronicle* furnishes further details—

A. 418. In the ninth year also, after the sacking of Rome by the Goths, those of Roman race who were left in Britain, not bearing the manifold insults of the people, bury their treasures in pits, thinking that hereafter they might have better fortune, which never was the case; and, taking a portion, assembled on the coasts, spread their canvass to the winds, and seek an exile on the shores of Gaul.

The "pass of the Ribble" is marked on the old map, published by Dr. Whitaker, with the crossed swords, indicative of a battle having been fought there, but this, though not unimportant in most cases, is of little value as evidence in favour of my hypothesis, inasmuch as, from its geographical position, it has, of necessity, often been the site of military conflicts, several of which are recorded in both local and other historical works.

The site now suggested agrees best, in a topographical sense, with the various descriptions of the conflict, the primary object of the war, and the necessary movements of the several combatants engaged. The great Roman road from the north passed through the county, and entered Cheshire at Latchford near Warrington. This road would serve both the invading Scots and Athelstan, and his army of West Saxons, Mercians, and other allies. A Roman road, from the Ribble and Wyre, called "Watling-street," crossed the country to York and the eastern coast. We have distinct information that Anlaf's great object was the re-conquest of the kingdom of Northumbria, and that, in the first instance, success crowned his efforts. Athelstan's two governors, Gudrekir and Alfgeirr, were defeated, and the former slain.

His colleague fled to his sovereign with the tidings of their discomfiture. The grandson of the Great Alfred immediately assembled his army and marched northward to confront in person his successful rival and his powerful allies. It appears, therefore, nearly absolutely certain that the struggle took place in Northumbria, or on its border, and, consequently other localities outside this region may almost be said to be "not in the hunt." Anlaf was the ruling chief of Dublin, and the virtual organizer and head of the confederacy. One wing of his army, according to Egil's saga, "was very numerous, and consisted of the disorderly Irish." The coast of Lancashire being part of the then Danish kingdom of Northumbria, was, in every respect, adapted for the landing of this portion of the invading army.

Hoveden, Mailros, and Simeon of Durham certainly say that Anlaf commenced the warfare by "entering the Humber with a fleet of 615 ships." This, however, may refer merely to the "*fleets of the warriors from Norway and the Baltic*," who joined in the confederacy. If Anlaf himself commanded this expedition in person, then he must have deputed the leadership of his "disorderly Irish" to one of his lieutenants. From an inspection of the map it will be found, after the defeat of Gudrekir and Alfgeirr, that the "pass of the Ribble," from a military point of view, was one of the most probable places at which the junction of the allies would take place. The Cumbrian Britons and the North and West Welsh could easily, by good Roman roads, join the Scottish monarch, as well as Anlaf's Irish troops and the warriors from Norway and the Baltic, at this spot, and dispute the passage of the fords with Athelstan's forces from the south. The "pass of the Ribble," from a topographical and military point of view, may therefore be assumed as very probably the site of the conflict.

I have previously referred to the fact that the name Brunanburh, in any corrupted form, is of little value in the present investigation without very strong supporting evidence, simply because so many localities have equal claim to it. The name itself is likewise variously written by the older writers when referring to the battle. It is termed *"Bellum Brune,"* or the "Battle of the Brune," in the *Brut y Tywysogion,* or the *Chronicle of the Princes of Wales,* and the *"Annales Cambria."* Henry of Huntingdon calls the locality Brunesburh; and the name is variously written by Geffrei Gaimar as Brunewerche, Brunewerce, and Brunewest. Ethelwerd, a contemporary chronicler, calls the place Brunandune. The author of Egil's saga calls the site Vinheid. Simeon of Durham says the battle was fought near Weondune or Ethrunnanwerch, or Brunnan byrge.

William of Malmesbury gives the name Brunsford, and Ingulph says Brunford in Northumbria. Notwithstanding the very important fact that the southern portion of the county of Lancaster suffered so much in the raids of Gilbert de Lacy and his soldiery after the Norman conquest, and the consequent non-productive character of much of the territory at the time of the Domesday survey, which caused very few names of places to be recorded in that valuable historical document, still I think present topographical nomenclature south of the "pass of the Ribble" sufficient to identify the locality from etymological evidence equal or superior in value to that yet advanced in favour of any other site. The word *brunan* means simply, in modern English, springs, and burh refers to any work of military defence of an artificial character. *Brun* has been corrupted, according to the conjectures of the authorities which I have previously cited, into *Burn, Brom, Brum, Broom, Bran, Ban, Bourne, Brink,* and *Brin.*

The name of the parish of Brindle, to the south-east of the "pass of the Ribble," has been written in various documents during the past few centuries, Burnhull, Brinhill, Brandhill, and, after becoming Brandle and Bryndhull, ends in its present Brindle. Now, burn and brun are acknowledged to be identical, the metathesis, as philologists term it, or transposition of the letter *r* under such circumstances being very common, especially in Lancashire. We say brid for bird, brun for burn, brunt for burnt, brast for burst, thurst for thrust, and some others. Birmingham is often called "Brummigem."

Indeed, Taylor, the "Water Poet," in his account of Old Parr, writes it "Brimicham." The short *u* with us is ofttimes sounded nearly like *i*, as in burst, burn, etc., like the German *ü* in Reüter, Müller, Prüssien, etc. Hence the interchangeability of brin for brun, of which the following are examples: The Icelandic Brynhildr, of the Eddaic poems, is the Brunhild of the Nibelungenlied; Brinsley, in Nottinghamshire, is sometimes written Brunsley; Burnside, near Kendal, was once Brynshead; Brynn, the seat of Lord Gerrard, between Wigan and Newton-in-Mackerfield, was, as I have shown in a previous chapter, anciently written Brun; and, in addition, I have recently seen, in Herman Moll's atlas, published in 1723, this same Brindle, south of Ribble, written Brunall, and, what is still further corroborative, in Christopher Saxton's much earlier map, published in Camden's *Britannia*, it is written Brundell, while Bryne and Burnley are spelled as at present.

Bryn or *bron* signifies a little hill, or the slope of a hill. As *burh* sometimes signifies a hill or eminence, as well as a fortification, the interchange of the British *bryn* with its Teutonic neighbour is in no way remarkable, but rather what might have been anticipated. Indeed, we find this phonetic substitution in Bernicia (the northern portion of Northumbria), the British equivalent being Bryneich. *Brunan*, as I have before said, signifies springs. Brindle church is situated on the slope of a hill, and the district, as a personal visit, or a glance at the six-inch ordnance map, will show, is remarkable for its numerous "wells," from which pure water issues from the surface of the ground. Dalton springs, Denham springs, and the well-known Whittle springs are in the neighbourhood, and one hamlet is named Manysprings.

In addition to Brindle we have Brinscall and Burnicroft, and Brownedge or Brunedge within the district. Between what I will now term Brunhull and Brunedge, we have the hamlet Bam*ber*, now termed Bamber Bridge. Baumber, in Lincolnshire, is sometimes written Bamburgh. Bramber, in Sussex, in Herman Moll's map (1723) is written Bamber, and in the Domesday survey Branber. Bromley, sometimes written Bramley, in Kent, is Brunlei, in the Domboc, and Bromborough, in Cheshire, is written Brunburgh, in Herman Moll's map. Hence if *bam* be likewise a corruption of brun, we have Brunberg, with Brunhull and Brunedge in immediate contiguity. The Rev. Jno. Whitaker and the Rev. E. Sibson say *bam* signifies war.

This is a very significant corruption, if a great battle were fought in its neighbourhood. Other authorities say *bam* means a "beam, a tree, a wood." This might imply that a fortification or stockade occupied the spot, or it might mean the fort in the wood, or in the neighbourhood of the wood, like the Welsh Bettws-y-coed. In Egil's saga "the wood" is often referred to in the detailed description of the battle. We have yet Worden-wood, Whittle-le-woods, Clayton-le-woods, and some others contiguous.

Kemble, in his (appendix) list of "patronymical names," which he regards as "those of ancient Marks," has two references, from the "Codex Diplomaticus," to "Bruningas," but he gives no conjecture as to the locality of its modern representative.

Mr. C. A. Weddle, of Wargrove, near Warrington, in 1857, when advocating the claims of Brunton, in Northumberland, after summing up the various names mentioned by the old writers, and referring to their evident corruption and variation, says—

> Two of them in particular, *Weardune and Wendune*, I have never seen noticed by any modern writer, yet *Weardune appears to me the most important name*, if Brunanburh be excepted, and even this is not more so. As to Wendune it is evidently a mistake in the transcribing for Werdune, the Anglo-Saxon *r* being merely *n*, with a long bottom stroke on the left.

Mr. Weddle finds a Warden Hill, about two miles from the farmhouse in "Chollerford field," in the neighbourhood of Brunton. This he considers as very conclusive evidence in favour of the locality being the Brunanburh of which we are in search. If such be the case, the existence of Wearden, or Worden, in the immediate neighbourhood of Brunhill, Bamber, and Brunedge, must unquestionably be more so, and especially when taken in connection with the large amount of corroborative evidence with which it is surrounded. The term Weardune is sometimes written Weondune, which, after the correction of the *n*, as suggested by Mr. Weddle, is Weorden. The ancient seat of the Faringtons, of Leyland and Farington, is variously written Werden, Worden, and Wearden, and it is pronounced by the inhabitants of the neighbourhood Wearden at the present day.

It must have been a place of some importance in the time of the Roman occupation. Many coins, and a heavy gold [3] signet ring, bearing the letters S P Q R, have been found there. The place is situated near the great Roman highway, and, if Anlaf's troops covered the "pass of the Ribble" near Brunhull, Brunburh and Brunedge, Wearden is precisely the neighbourhood where Athelstan's forces, coming from the south, would encamp in front of them. Dr. Kuerden, upwards of

---

3. Mr. Thompson Watkins, *His. Soc. Trans.,* says the metal is bronze.

two centuries ago, describes the northern boundary of the township of Euxton-burgh as the "Werden broke." Mr. Baines states that there is in Leyland churchyard "a stone of the 14th century, covering all that remains of the Weardens of Golden Hill." It is highly probable that the present Cuerden is itself a corruption of Wearden. The prefix Cuer is found in Cuerden, Cuerdale (where the great hoard was found), and Cuerdley near Prescot, and in no other part of England.

The names in the locality, as I have previously said, are not recorded in the Domesday survey, but the Norman-French generally represented the English sound *w* by *gu*. Philologists regard the consonants *c*, *q*, *ch*, and *g*, as "identical" or "convertible," consequently, if I assume the initial *C* in Cuerden to be equivalent to *G*, we have a Norman-French method of writing Wearden. That *cu* was used to represent the sound of our *w*, is demonstrated by a reference to the survey itself, for in the Domesday record, Fishwick, now a portion of the borough of Preston, and situated on the opposite bank of the Ribble to Cuerdale, is actually written Fiscuic. Leland, too, in his Itinerary, spells the River Cocker indifferently with the initials C, G, and K. The district in the parish of Leyland, anciently styled *Cunnolvesmores*, is sometimes found written *Gunoldsmores*.

Simeon of Durham says the battle was fought near Weondune, or *Ethrunanwerch*, or Brunan byrge. I have never seen any attempt to identify this Ethrunanwerch with any modern locality in any part of the country. There is no such name to be found now, nor anything suggestive of it, in a gazetteer of England and Wales, and I therefore presume that it has either entirely disappeared or become so altered as to be unrecognizable. Consequently, if I fail in an attempt to identify it, not much injury will result therefrom. The termination *werch* presents no difficulty. It is evidently *worth*, as in Saddleworth, Shuttleworth, etc., and could easily give place to some other suffix indicating residence or occupation, or even locality. The prefix Ethrunan is more difficult to deal with, and I should perhaps not have attempted its solution, if I had not seen on a map the name Rother applied to one of the head waters which, uniting near Stockport, form the Mersey. This stream is generally called the Etherow.[4]

This is the nearest approach to Ethrunan that I have been able to meet with. If *rother*, by a kind of metathesis, is an equivalent to *ether*, perhaps I can detect two distinct remains of the word Ethrunanwerch,

---

4. In Herman Moll's map, the Etherow, before its junction with the Goyt and Tame, is written Mersey.

in the neighbourhood of Wearden. On the ordnance map we have, about a mile from Werden Hall, Rotherham Top, and a stream, recently diverted for the purpose of the Liverpool water supply, named the Roddlesworth. This word implies a place on the bank of a stream, and as the *d* and *th* are phonetic equivalents, it may be read Rothelsworth or Ethrunlesworth; indeed, Mr. Baines expressly says, "Withnall, or Withnell, also a part of the lordship of Gunoldsmores, containing Rothelsworth, a name derived from Roddlesworth, or Mouldenwater, a rapid stream."

On the one-inch to the mile ordnance map there is a name which preserves the form of the first part of the word without the transposition, or metathesis, to which I have referred. Not far from Worden Hall is a small hamlet named "Ethrington." The fact that these names exist in the neighbourhood strengthens the probability that the etymology is not altogether fanciful, and consequently lends support to the presumption that the locality suggested may be the true site of Athelstan's great victory.

I have said that there are several places in Lancashire, even, which answer to Brunan or Brun. The following are amongst the number: On the Wyre, near the commencement of the Roman agger or "*Danes' Pad*," as it is locally termed, which led from the Portus Setantiorum of Ptolemy to York, is a place named Bourne, written in the Domesday survey Brune. Bourne Hall is situated upon a "dune" or hill, which commands a relatively recently blocked up channel of the Wyre. Therefore Brunnandune or Brunford would strictly apply to it. Bryning-with-Kellamergh, near *Warton*, in the parish of Kirkham, is described in a charter of the reign of John, as Brichscrach *Brun* and Kelmers*burgh*. In the time of Henry III. it is described as Brininge.

Not far from Rochdale is a spot named "Kildanes," near Bamford. The site is not much more than two miles from a place named Burnedge or Brunedge. There is a Burnage between Manchester and Stockport. Burnley is situated on the River Burn, generally, however, called the Brun. This demonstrates how utterly impossible it is to identify the locality by the name Brunanburh. The Manchester, Rochdale, and Burnley sites are too far from the seashore. The fine old poem, describing the battle, says emphatically—

There were made flee the Northman's chieftain, By need constrained, To the ship's prow, With a little band. The *bark* drove afloat—The king departed—On the fallow flood his life he preserved.

The Northmen departed In their nailed barks; Bloody relic of darts; On roaring ocean, O'er the deep water, Dublin to seek; Again Ireland shamed in mind.

West Saxons onwards Throughout the day, In numerous bands, Pursued the footsteps of the loathed nations.

I therefore contend that, in this particular, as well as those already disposed of, the "pass of the Ribble" answers to the locality of the struggle, as described by contemporary authority. Where this topographical feature is wanting, I hold it to be fatal. The ships of Anlaf might be attending the army in the estuaries of the Ribble or Wyre, and to them the defeated and routed forces would, of course, repair with headlong speed, after crossing the fords, the defence of which they had so gallantly, if unsuccessfully, attempted. During this hasty retreat, I contend it is highly probable the great Cuerdale hoard was deposited, and, owing to death, or other disaster, the precise locality could not be determined in after times, although the tradition of its deposition remained.

There is plenty of analagous evidence in support of such a conjecture, to some of which I have already referred. In the seventh volume of *Collectania Antiqua*, Mr. Charles Roach Smith, referring to the then recent discovery near the Roman station, "*Procolitia*," near the great Roman Wall, of an enormous mass (15,000) of Roman coins, weighing about 400 pounds, says he regards the hoard as part of the money set apart for the payment of the troops occupying the adjoining *castrum*, which, *owing to some sudden panic in the reign of Gratian*, was concealed in the well or fountain dedicated to a local divinity, Conesstina. The *Saxon Chronicle*, as well as Ethelwerd, as I have already stated, refer to the burying of treasure under similar circumstances. The former says—

This year (*A.D.* 418) the Romans collected all the treasures that were in Britain, and some they hid in the earth, so that no one has since been able to find them, and some they carried with them into Gaul.

Athelstan's connection with Preston and its neighbourhood, at the head of his army, is attested by stronger evidence than mere tradition. In the year 930 he granted the whole of the hundred of Amounderness to the cathedral church at York. He is said to have "*purchased*" the territory with his own money, a somewhat remarkable financial operation for a conquering king in the tenth century, in Anglo-Saxon and Pagan Danish times. But perhaps a previous grant to the church at Ripon influenced him in this matter.

In the early part of the seventeenth century lived one William Elston, who, in a MS. entitled, *Mundana Mutabilia, or Ethelestophylax*, now in the Harleian collection in the British Museum, placed upon record the following interesting particulars relative to this monarch—

> It was once told me by Mr. Alexander Elston, who was uncle to my father and sonne to Ralph Elston, my great grandfather, that the said Ralph Elston had a deede or a copy of a deede in the Saxon tongue, wherein it did appear that king *Ethelstan lying in camp in this county upon occacon of warres*, gave the land of Ethelston vnto one to whom himself was Belsyre. (godfather).

The township of Elston, in the parish of Preston, formerly written Ethelstan, is situated on the north bank of the Ribble a little above Cuerdale and Red Scar.

To the south of Brindle and the east of Worden, near Whittle Springs, is a large *tumulus*, and the hill side on which it is situated has the appearance of having been, at some time, disturbed by human agency. A Roman vicinal way, from Wigan to Blackburn, or Mellor, where it joins the main highway from Manchester to Ribchester, passes near it. Remains of this road were discovered near Adlington not many years ago. Another ancient road, probably of similar origin, leaves the main Roman military way from Warrington to Lancaster at Bamberbridge, and running in the direction of Manchester, crosses this in its neighbourhood. This *tumulus* is named "Pickering Castle;" which has an important significance. *Tumuli* are often termed "castles." We have the "Castle Hill" near Newton-in-Mackerfield, and the "Castle Hill" at Penwortham, near Preston.

The *tumulus* near to "Whittle Springs" is very similar to these in appearance, and may, on excavation, prove to be a sepulchral mound. Pickering, according to the method of interpretation adopted by John Mitchell Kemble, in his *Saxons in England*, should indicate the "Mark" of a sept or clan bearing that name, like the Faringas as at Farington, Billingas as at Billington, and many others. But there is not the slightest reference by any writer of such a name ever holding property in the neighbourhood, and Mr. Kemble places the Pickering, in Yorkshire, only among the probable instances, as he had never met with any account of a Saxon family or mark answering to it.

As the letters *P* and *V* are interchangeable sounds, "vikingring" has been suggested as the original form of the word. Dr. Smith, in his annotations to Marsh's *Lectures on the English Languages,* speaks of the "Danes being led by the Vikings, the younger sons of their royal houses." As the old poem says—

Five kings lay on the battle-stead.
Youthful kings
By swords in slumber laid.
So seven eke
Of Anlaf's earls,
Of the army countless.

This interpretation seems not improbable; yet it may be no more than an accidental coincidence rather than a legitimate derivation. As *P* and *B* are equally interchangeable consonants, I am inclined to think that "Bickering Castle" may have been the original name of the tumulus. *Bicra,* in the modern Welsh, means to fight, from whence our word *bickering.* In this case, *ing* meaning field, the interpretation would be the "Castle of the Battlefield."

There is some good analogy in support of this view. Mr. Thos. Baines, in his *Lancashire and Cheshire: Past and Present,* says—

The *Peck*forton Hills extend from Beeston Castle to the Dee. On one of them *Bicker*ton Hill, 500 feet high, is a strong camp with a double line of earthworks. One front overlooks the plain of Cheshire. The earthwork is called the "Maiden Castle."

Not far from Bickerton Hill is Bickley, where, according to Ormerod, certain brass tablets were recently discovered, recording a grant of the freedom of the city of Rome to certain troops serving in Britain in the reign of Trajan, *A.D.* 98-117, some of whom may have been stationed in the neighbourhood where the tablets were found. We have in Lancashire the township of Bickerstaffe, and an adjoining wood named Bickershaw. Bickerstaffe was anciently written Bicker-*stat* and Bykyr*stath.* Stadt, stad, or stead means a station or settlement. Thus we have battle-wood and battle-stead. We have seen that the old poem says—*Five kings lay on the battle-stead, youthful kings, by swords in slumber laid.* Besides, we find Bicker and Bickering in Lincolnshire, and Bickerton in both Northumberland and the East Riding of Yorkshire. Whatever this may be worth, it is most desirable that this *tumulus* should be dug into, for remains might, and probably would, be found which could throw additional light upon the subject of the present investigation.

In the yard of Brindle Parish Church, beneath the chancel window, is an ancient stone coffin, with a circular hollow for the head of the corpse. Nothing further is known respecting it, beyond that it was dug up somewhere in the neighbourhood, and had been removed to its present position with a view to its preservation.

In 1867 I examined the Ancient British burial mound and its contents, then recently discovered in the park land attached to Whitehall, and contiguous to that of Low Hill House, the residence of Mr. Ellis Shorrock, at Over Darwen, and contributed a paper respecting it to the *Transactions of the Lancashire and Cheshire Historic Society*. In that paper I say—

> I heard that there is a tradition, yet implicitly relied on, which speaks of a battle fought in the olden time somewhere in the neighbourhood of Tockholes in the Roddlesworth valley, and stories that remains, including those of horses, have been found, which are believed to confirm it. Respecting this I may have something to say in a future paper.

What I have to say is this: that if a severe struggle took place near the *tumulus* to which I have referred, the routed army, following the Roman vicinal way to Ribchester, would pass by the locality, which is not far distant. This adds another link in the chain of evidence by which I have sought to demonstrate that the *most probable* site of Athelstan's great victory at Brunanburh is that which I have indicated near the famous "pass of the Ribble," to the south of Preston, and that the great Cuerdale hoard of treasure was buried on the bank of the stream, during the disastrous retreat of the routed confederate armies.

In the appendix to the *History of Preston and its Environs*, published in 1857, after discussing Mr. Weddle's objections to a Lancashire site, I concluded with the following words—

> These reasons, in conjunction with those advanced in the second chapter of this work, induce the author to prefer the locality, in the present state of the evidence, as the *most probable* site of the 'Battle of the Brun.'

Although the evidence advanced in its favour on the present occasion is considerably in excess of that previously obtainable, I still merely reassert my previous conviction, without dogmatism, that, on weighing the whole of the evidence yet adduced, I am justified in maintaining that the site I name is the *most probable* which has yet been suggested; indeed, there is very little reliable evidence in favour of any other. But, in conclusion, I again reiterate what I wrote twenty-five years ago, when dealing with the Roman topography of the county, that "no permanent settlement of so difficult a question ought to be insisted upon, until every means of investigation and all the resources of logical inference have been fairly exhausted."

I have already said that the neighbourhood of Preston and "the pass of the Ribble," as might have been expected from its topographical position, and consequent strategical importance, has been the scene of many known conflicts. Robert Bruce, in 1323, burned the town, but ventured no further southward. Holinshed says he "entered into England, by Carlisle, kept on his way through Cumberland, Westmoreland, and Lancaster, to Preston, which town he burnt, as he had done others in the counties he had passed through, and, after three weeks and three days, he returned into Scotland without engaging."

Dr. Kuerden, writing shortly before the guild of 1682, laments the destruction of documentary evidence relating to this famous Preston festival during the turmoil of civil war. After enumerating the dates of those still preserved, in his day, in the Corporation records, he says—

> These are such as doth appeare within the records and gild books, that yet remain extant and in being, though some I conceive to be omitted, as one gild in Henry 6th dayes occasion'd, as I conceive, in those distractions and civil wars betwixt the Houses of Lancaster and York; another gild merchant omitted to be kept in K. H. 8th dayes, occasioned, as may be thought, by the revolutions at that time in church affayres; the next that are wanting may be through the loss of records in K. Edw. 3rd dayes [*sic.*] wheras the Scottish army burnt the burrough of Preston to the very ground.

Kuerden is in error with reference to the king's reign in which this disaster occurred; Bruce's foray took place in the reign of Edward II. In the *History of Preston and its Environs*, I say—

> A tradition still remains that Roman Ribchester was destroyed by an earthquake; another that it was reduced to ashes in the early part of the fourteenth century, during the great inroad of the Scots under Bruce. Both are highly improbable. Had Ro-

161

man Ribchester remained a place of any importance till the period referred to, it could scarcely have failed to have attracted the notice of some of the elder chroniclers or topographers. True, the *Saxon village* may have shared the fate of Preston, in the celebrated foray of our northern neighbours, and hence the tradition! An earthquake in England, of sufficient magnitude to bury a Roman 'city,' (to use the elder Whitaker's emphatic style,) '*must*' have found someone to record it. Other facts, however, demonstrate that this tradition can have no better foundation than the vague conjecture of ignorant peasants; who, on first discovering remains of ancient buildings beneath the soil, naturally attributed their subterranean location to the action of some earthquake, in that mysterious period usually denominated the 'olden time.'

In Leland's day, the remains of the Roman temple dedicated to Minerva were believed to have been connected with Jewish religious rites and ceremonies, from the simple fact that they knew of no other non-Christian sect with whom to associate them.

At the commencement of the campaign in 1643 between Charles I. and the Parliament, General Fairfax, from his headquarters at Manchester, ordered an attack upon Preston, then garrisoned by the king's troops. The town was at that time fortified by "inner and outer walls of brick," no vestige of which now remains, although it was recently not very difficult to trace their site. The command was entrusted to General Sir John Seaton. Captain Booth led the attack, and scaled the outer wall. The garrison defended the inner wall with great valour, "with push of pike," until Sir John Seaton, having stormed the defences on the eastern side, entered the town by Church-street, when they were overpowered, and the Parliamentary army obtained complete possession of the town, but not before the mayor, Adam Morte, and his son, had fallen in the conflict.

Colonel Rosworm, the celebrated Parliamentary engineer, afterwards refortified the town. Shortly afterwards Major-General Seaton and Colonel Ashton marched from Preston, with the view to relieve Lancaster, then besieged by the Earl of Derby. The earl drew off his troops on their approach, and falling suddenly on Preston, in its then defenceless state, stormed the works in three places. After an hour's severe fighting the place surrendered. Lord Derby secured the magazine, and destroyed the military works, fearing the place might again fall into the enemy's hands.

In August, 1664, a smart little struggle took place at Ribble Bridge, which Colonel Shuttleworth thus describes in his dispatch—

> Right Honourable,—Upon Thursday last, marching with three of my troops upon Blackburn towards Preston, where the ennemie lay, I met eleven of their colours at Ribble Bridge, within a mile of Preston, whereupon, after a sharp fight, we took the Lord Ogleby, a Scotch Lord, Colonel Ennis, one other colonel slaine, one major wounded, and divers officers and soldiers to the number of forty in all taken, besides eight or nine slaine, with the losse of twelve men taken prisoners, which afterwards were released by Sir John Meldrum upon his coming to Preston the night following, from whence the enemy fled.

Four years afterwards, Cromwell achieved his great victory over the Duke of Hamilton and the Marquis of Langdale. Reference has been made, in the previous chapter, to the rapid march of the Parliamentary forces from Skipton, by Clitheroe, to Stonyhurst, where they encamped on the evening of August 16th, 1648. Some difference respecting the then famous "Covenant" prevented Langdale's forces from combining heartily with those of the Duke. His English troops were encamped on Ribbleton Moor, to the east of Preston. Hamilton's Scotch forces were widely scattered. Some of his advanced horse lay at Wigan; his main army occupied Preston, while his rear, under Monro, were in the neighbourhood of Garstang. Short work was made, notwithstanding the great numerical superiority, with such discipline and divided councils, by a soldier of Cromwell's calibre.

In the words of Thomas Carlyle, he "dashed in upon him, cut him in two, drove him north *and* south, into as miserable ruin as his worst enemy could wish." "The bridge of Ribble" was fiercely contested. When the Parliamentary troops, with "push of pike" (Cromwell's equivalent for the modern phrase "*at the point of the bayonet*"), at length prevailed, the duke's army retreated over the Darwen, which joins the Ribble in the immediate neighbourhood. Night put an end to the conflict. Before daylight the Royalist army decamped, but was hotly pursued, through Chorley, Wigan, and Warrington, into the midland counties, and rapidly destroyed. The Duke of Hamilton was taken prisoner at Uttoxeter, and a similar fate befell Langdale at Nottingham.[5]

This victory is celebrated as one of Cromwell's greatest military

---

5. For details of this battle see *History of Preston and its Environs.*

achievements, by Milton, in his famous sonnet:—

To The Lord General Cromwell.

Cromwell, our chief of men, who, through a cloud
Not of war only, but detractions rude,
Guided by faith and matchless fortitude,
To peace and truth thy glorious way has plough'd,
And on the neck of crowned Fortune proud
Hast reared God's trophies and his work pursued,
While Darwen stream with blood of Scots imbued,
And Dunbar field resound thy praises loud,
And Worcester's laureat wreath. Yet much remains
To conquer still; Peace hath her victories
No less renown'd than War; new foes arise
Threat'ning to bind our souls with secular chains:
Help us to save free conscience from the paw
Of hireling wolves, whose gospel is their maw.

The number of the troops engaged in this short but brilliant campaign is stated variously by different authorities. There is an entry in the records of the Corporation of Preston which says

Decimo Septimo die Augustie, 1648, 24 Car,—That Henry Blundell, gent., being mayor of this town of Preston, the daie and yeare aforesaid, Oliver Cromwell, lieutenant-general of the forces of the Parliament of England, with an army of about 10,000 at the most, (whereof 1500 were Lancashire men, under the command of Colonel Ralph Assheton, of Middleton), fought a battail in and about Preston aforesaid, and over-threw Duke Hamilton, general of the Scots, consisting of about 26,000, and of English, Sir Marmaduke Langdale and his forces, joined with the Scots, about 4,000; took all their ammunition, about 3,000 prisoners, killed many with very small losse to the parliament army; and in their pursuit towards Lancaster, Wigan, Warrington, and divers other places in Cheshire, Staffordshire, and Nottinghamshire, took the said Duke and Langdale, with many Scottish earls and lords, and about 10,000 prisoners more, all being taken (or) slayne, few escaping, and all their treasure and plunder taken. This performed in less than one week.

Captain Hodgson notices the plundering propensities of the enemy, but, as we have seen in the previous chapter, he entertained no higher an opinion of his Lancashire allies, with respect to their "looting" proclivities. His estimate of the numbers of the army of the Parliament is somewhat less than that in the Corporation record. He says—

> The Scots marched towards Kendal, we towards Rippon; where Oliver met us with horse and foot. We were then betwixt eight and nine thousand; a fine smart army, and fit for action. We marched up to Skipton; and the forlorn of the enemy's horse was come to Gargrave, and took some men away, and made others pay what money they pleased; having made havock in the country, it seems intending never to come there again.

Cromwell, in his despatch "to the Honourable William Lenthall, Esquire, Speaker of the House of Commons," dated "Warrington, 20th August, 1648," of course attributes all the honour and glory to the Almighty, yet, modestly enough, he claims some credit as due to the Parliamentary army, if it rested merely upon the disparity in the number of the combatants. He says—

> Thus you have a narrative of the particulars of the success which God hath given you; which I could hardly at this time have done, considering the multiplicity of business, but truly, when I was once engaged in it, I could hardly tell how to say less, there being so much of God in it; and I am not willing to say more, lest there should seem to be any of man. Only give me leave to add one word, showing the disparity of forces on both sides, that you may see, and all the world acknowledge, the great hand of God in this business.
>
> The Scots army could not be less than twelve thousand effective foot, well armed, and five thousand horse; Langdale not less than two thousand five hundred foot, and fifteen hundred horse; in all twenty-one-thousand: and truly very few of their foot but were as well armed if not better than yours, and at divers disputes did fight two or three hours before they would quit their ground. Yours were about two thousand five hundred horse and dragoons of your old army; about four thousand foot of your old army; also about sixteen hundred Lancashire foot, and about five hundred Lancashire horse; in all about eight thousand six hundred. You see by computation about two thousand of the enemy slain; betwixt eight and nine thousand prisoners; besides what are lurking in hedges and private places, which the county daily bring in or destroy.

Notwithstanding the great social and political importance of this victory, and the renown of the general by whom it was achieved, whose very name is yet associated in the minds of some with every odious moral feature, and, in the judgment of others, with the highest English statesmanship, unselfish patriotism, and sincere religious conviction, the amount of legendary story which it has left behind is singularly limited. I have heard of several localities in Lancashire, and some neighbouring counties, where tradition records that Oliver Cromwell once visited the district and slept in some specified house or mansion, although there exists not the slightest reliable evidence that Oliver was ever in the neighbourhood. This, in some instances, I fancy, may be accounted for by the fact that Cromwell's name has become a typical or generic one, and has done duty for nearly a couple of centuries with the public generally, for every commander, either generals or subordinate officers, belonging to the Parliamentary armies.

One tradition, however, was well-known in my youthful days. The mound planted with trees on "Walton Flats" was always regarded as "the grave of the Scotch warriors." The place was rather a solitary one at night, and some superstitious fear was often confessed by others than children, when passing it after nightfall. It was in this mound, in 1855, whilst looking for remains of the said "Scotch warriors," that I came upon evidences of Roman occupation. Faith in the legend was attested when one of the workmen informed me that he had found in the mound a halfpenny with the figure of a Scotchman in the place of Britannia, on the reverse. I found it to be a Roman second brass coin, the military costume of a soldier suggesting to the labourer a kilted Highlander.

Although at various times relics of the fight have been picked up, they are now extremely rare. The flood waters of the Ribble have occasionally dislodged human bones, including skulls, from the banks, and these are almost universally, if somewhat vaguely, associated with "Scotch warriors," but without any definite notion as to the period or cause of their presence in the neighbourhood. I remember, many years ago, suggesting to a very old man employed on a rope-walk near the south bank of the river, that, as a number of English, including some Lancashire men, were slain in the great battle in 1648, it was possible a portion of the bones might belong to them. He did not deny the *possibility*; but simply remarked that he had never heard the remains attributed to any but the aforesaid "Scotch warriors;" and he was evidently, from his point of view, too "patriotic" to entertain, himself, the slightest doubt on the subject.

A Protestant minister of Annandale, a Mr. Patten, who accompanied the Stuart army, and published a *History of the Rebellion* in 1715, condemns the Jacobite leaders for not defending the "Pass of the Ribble." The approach to the old bridge down the steep incline from Preston was by a lane, which was, he says, "very deep indeed." This lane was situated about midway between the present road and the hollow, yet visible, by which the Roman road passed to the north. He adds—

> This is that famous lane at the end of which Oliver Cromwell met with a stout resistance from the King's forces, who from the height rolled down upon him and his men (when they had entered the lane) huge large millstones; and if Oliver himself had not forced his horse to jump into a quicksand, he had luckily ended his days there.

Commenting on this passage in the *History of Preston*, I say—

> Notwithstanding Mr. Patten's political conversion *afterwards*, and his horror of the 'licentious freedom' of those who 'cry up the old doctrines of passive obedience, and give hints and arguments to prove hereditary right,' he appears to have retained all the antipathy of a Stuart partisan to the memory of Oliver Cromwell. Yet the loyalty of 1648 became rebellion in 1715, when Mr. Patten's head was in danger. Such is the mutation of human dogmatism.

Cromwell, in a letter to the Solicitor-General, "his worthy friend, Oliver St. John, Esquire," shortly after the battle, relates an incident which illustrates one of the phases of religious thought amongst our Puritan ancestors, and which is by no means extinct at the present time. He says—

> I am informed from good hands, that a poor godly man died in Preston, the day before the fight; and being sick, near the hour of his death, he desired the woman that cooked to him, to fetch him a handful of grass. She did so; and when he received it, he asked, whether it would wither or not, now it was cut? The woman said 'yea.' He replied, 'So should this Army of the Scots do, and come to nothing, so soon as ours did but appear,' or words to this effect, and so immediately died.

Thomas Carlyle's old Puritan blood is up, as he contemplates the possibility of some adverse critic citing this story as evidence of Cromwell's intellectual weakness, or, at least, of his proneness to superstition. He almost fiercely exclaims—

> Does the reader look with any intelligence into that poor old prophetic, symbolic, Death-bed scene at Preston? Any intelligence of Prophecy and Symbol, in general; of the symbolic Man-child *Mahershalal-hashbaz* at Jerusalem, or the handful of Cut Grass at Preston—of the opening Portals of Eternity, and what departing gleams there are in the Soul of the pure and the just? Mahershalal-hashbaz ('Hasten-to-the-spoil,' so called), and the bundle of Cut Grass are grown somewhat strange to us! Read; and having sneered duly,—consider.

In August, 1651, Colonel Lilburne defeated the Earl of Derby at Wigan-lane, in which engagement the gallant Major-general Sir Thomas Tildesley fell. On the day previous to the battle, a skirmish took place between the Royalists and the Parliamentary troops at the "pass of the Ribble." In his letter to Cromwell, Lilburne says—

"The next day, in the afternoone, I having not foot with me, a party of the Enemies Horse fell smartly amongst us where our Horses were grazing, and for some space put us pretty hard to it; but at last it pleased the Lord to strengthen us so as that we put them to flight, and pursued them to *Ribble-bridge*, (this was something like our business at *Mussleburgh*), and kild and tooke about 30 prisoners, most Officers and Gentlemen, with the loss of two men that dyed next morning; but severall wounded, and divers of our good Horses killed."

Anno Domini 1715. "Time's whirligig" hath brought about strange changes. A "Restoration" and a "Glorious Revolution" have passed across the stage. The faithful followers of the dethroned Stuarts, the "royalists" of the last century, have been transformed into the "rebels" of this. The partisans of Prince James Francis Edward Stuart, styled the "Elder Pretender," after a successful march from Scotland, arrived at Preston, and took possession of the town.

The "Chevalier" was proclaimed king. Brigadier Macintosh was anxious to defend the "pass" at Ribble-bridge, but, as the previous fortifications of the town had been destroyed, it was determined instead to barricade the entrance to the principal streets. The town was besieged for two days by Generals Wills and Carpenter. After a brave defence, notwithstanding the incompetency of "General" Forster, the partisans of the Stuart were compelled to surrender at discretion.[5]

In 1745, Prince Charles Edward, or the "Young Pretender," as he was styled, marched from Scotland on his way to Derby, through Preston; and again, a little more expeditiously on his return therefrom.

Mr. Robert Chambers says—

"The clansmen had a superstitious dread, in consequence of the misfortunes of their party at Preston, in 1715, that they would never get beyond this town; to dispel the illusion, Lord George Murray crossed the Ribble, and quartered a number of men on the other side."

A single repulse could scarcely justify such foreboding. The name of the Ribble had evidently become associated with previous disasters, as well as with the relatively recent surrender of the Scotch and English forces under Forster, Derwentwater, and Macintosh in 1715.

Considering the many exquisite poetical effusions which the misfortunes of the Stuarts added to Scottish literature, it is surprising that nothing, but some of the veriest doggrels in relation thereto, can be met with on the southern side of the border. *Brigadier Macintosh's Farewell to the Highlands* is beneath criticism, and *Long Preston Peggy to Proud Preston went* is not much better. In May, 1847, a story appeared in *New Tales of the Borders and the British Isles*.

It is introduced by the first *stanza* of the ballad. The scene is laid at Walton-le-dale and Preston, 1815. It is a sad jumble of fact and fiction. It confounds with one another events in the campaigns of 1715 and 1745, and illustrates, to some extent, the confusion of history and artistic fiction discussed in the preceding pages of this work. Peggy, who, in her old age, after a somewhat profuse indulgence in ardent spirits, had still some remains of a handsome face and fine person, frequently sung the song of which she was the heroine, five and twenty years after the occurrence of the events which gave rise to it. (See note following).

Note:—Mr. J. P. Morris, in *Notes and Queries*, says—
Many collectors have endeavoured, but in vain, to find more of this old Lancashire ballad than the two verses given by Dr. Dixon, in his *Songs and Ballads of the English Peasantry*, and by Mr. Harland, in his *Ballads and Songs of Lancashire*. I have much pleasure in forwarding to *Notes and Queries* the following ver-

---

5. For details respecting this siege, see *His. Preston, c. v.*

sion, which is much more complete than any yet given:

Long Preston Peggy to Proud Preston went,
To view the Scotch Rebels it was her intent;
A noble Scotch lord, as he passed by,
On this Yorkshire damsel did soon cast an eye.

He called to his servant, who on him did wait—
'Go down to yon maiden who stands in the gate,
That sings with a voice so soft and so sweet,
And in my name do her lovingly greet.'

So down from his master away he did hie,
For to do his bidding, and bear her reply;
But ere to this beauteous virgin he came,
He moved his bonnet, not knowing her name.

'It's, oh! Mistress Madame, your beauty's adored,
By no other person than by a Scotch lord,
And if with his wishes you will comply,
All night in his chamber with him you shall lie.'

Appendix

The Disposal of St. Oswald's Remains

Mr. John Ingram, in his *Claimants to Royalty*, referring to the defeat of Don Sebastian, King of Portugal, in 1578, by the Moors, says—

After the fight, a corse, recognised by one of the survivors as the king's, was discovered by the victorious Moors, and forwarded by the Emperor of Morocco as a present to his ally, Philip the Second of Spain. In 1583, this monarch restored it to the Portuguese, by whom it was interred with all due solemnity in the royal mausoleum in the church of Our Lady of Belem.

It thus seems that Dean Howson's conjecture, referred to in chapter 2, is, at least, not without precedent.

The Dun Bull, the Badge of the Nevilles.

Mr. W. Brailsford, in *The Antiquary* (August, 1882), referring to the marriage which united the properties of the Bulmers and the Nevilles, in 1190, says—

The dun bull, which is the badge of the Norman Nevilles, was in reality derived from the Saxon Bulmers, though it has been thought by some antiquarian searchers to have had its origin from the wild cattle which, once on a time, like those still existing at Chillingham, roamed in the park here, then and at a later date.

The Genesis of Myths.

When the preceding pages were nearly all in type, I ordered a copy of the then just published essay entitled *Myth and Science*, by Signor Tito Vignoli, in which the gradual development of mythic thought and expression is expounded with great clearness and precision. He says:

Doubtless it is difficult for us to picture for ourselves the psychical conditions of primitive men, at a time when the objects of perception and the apprehension of things were presented by an effort of memory to the mind as if they were actual and living things, yet such conditions are not hypothetical, but really existed, as any one may ascertain for himself who is able to realise that primitive state of mind, and we have said enough to show that such was its necessary condition.

The fact becomes more intelligible when we consider man, and especially the uneducated man, under the exciting influence of any passion, and how at such times he will, even when alone, gesticulate, speak aloud, and reply to internal questions which he imagines to be put to him by absent persons, against whom he is at the moment infuriated; the images of these persons and things are, as it were, present and in agitation within him; and these images, in the fervour of emotion and under the stimulus of excitement, appear to be actually alive, although only presented to the inward psychical consciousness.

In the natural man, in whom the intellectual powers were very slowly developed, the animation and personification effected by his mind and consciousness were threefold: first of the objects themselves as they really existed, then of the idea or image corresponding to them in the memory, and lastly of the specific types of these objects and images. There was within him a vast and continuous drama, of which we are no longer conscious, or only retain a faint and distant echo, but which is partly revealed by a consideration of the primitive value of words and their roots in all languages. The meaning of these, which is now for the most part lost and unintelligible, always expressed a material and concrete fact, or some gesture. This is true of classic tongues, and is well known to all educated people, and it recurs in the speech of all savage and barbarous races.

Ia Rau is used to express *all* in the Marquesas Isles. *Rau* signifies *leaves*, so that the term implies something as numerous as the leaves of a tree. *Rau* is also now used for *sound*, an expression which includes in itself the conception of *all*, but which originally signified a fact, a real and concrete phenomenon, and it was felt as such in the ancient speech in which it was used in this sense. So again in Tahiti *huru*, *ten*, originally signified *hairs*; *rima*, *five*, was at first used for *hand*; *riri*, *anger*, literally means *he shouts. Uku* in the Marquesas Isles means *to lower the head,* and is now used for *to enter a house. Kùku,* which had the same original name in New Zealand, now expresses the act of diving.

The Polynesian word *toro* at first indicated anything in the position of a hand with extended fingers, whence comes the Tahitian term for ox, *puaátoro, stretching pig,* in allusion to the way in which an ox carries his head. *Toó* (Marquesas), to put forward the hand, is now used for *to take. Tongo* (Marquesas), to grope with extended arms, leads to *protongo tongo, darkness.* In New Zealand, *wairua,* in Tahiti*varua,* signifies soul or spirit, from *vai,* to remain in a recumbent position, and *rua,* two; that is *to be in two places,* since they believed that in sickness or in dreams the soul left the body.[1] Throughout Polynesia, *moe* signifies a recumbent position or to sleep, and in Tahiti *moe pipiti* signifies a double sleep or dream, from*moe,* to sleep, and *piti,* two. In New Zealand, *moenaku* means to try to grasp something during sleep; from *naku,* to take in the fingers.

We can understand something of the mysterious exercise of human intelligence in its earliest development from this habit of symbolizing and presenting in an outward form an abstract conception, thus giving a concrete meaning and material expression to the external fact. We see how everything assumed a concrete, living form, and can better understand the conditions we have established as necessary in the early days of the development of human life. This attitude of the intelligence had been often stated before, but in an incomplete way; the primitive and subsequent myths have been confounded together; [See *ante, p.p. 44, et seq., et 116*] and it has been supposed that myth was of exclusively human origin, whereas it has its roots lower down in the vast animal kingdom.

Anthropomorphism, and the personification of the things and phenomena of nature, and their images and specific types, were the great source whence issued superstitions, mythologies, and religions, and, also, as we shall presently see, the scientific errors to be found among all the families of the human race.

For the development of myth, which is in itself always a human personification of natural objects and phenomena in some form or other, the first and necessary foundation consists, as we have abundantly shown, in the conscious and deliberate

---

1. See Gaussin's *Langue Polynésienne.*

vivification of objects by the perception and apprehension of animals. And since this is a condition of animal perception, it is also the foundation of all human life, and of the spontaneous and innate exercise of the intelligence. In fact, man, by a two-fold process, raises above his animal nature a world of images, ideas, and conceptions from the types he has formed of various phenomena, and his attitude towards this internal world does not differ from his attitude towards that which is external. He personifies the images, ideas, and conceptions, by transforming them into living subjects, just as he had originally personified cosmic objects and phenomena.

This was the source of primitive, confused, and inorganic fetishism among all peoples; namely, that they ascribed intentional and conscious life to a host of natural objects and phenomena. Hence came the fears, the adoration, the guardianship of, or abhorrence for, some given species of stones, plants, animals, some strange forms or unusual natural object. The subsequent adoration of idols and images, all sorts of talismans, the virtue of relics, dreams, incantations and exorcisms, had the same origin, and were all due to this primitive genesis of the fetish. the internal duplication of the external animation and personification of objects.

Anglo-Saxon Helmet

The remains of a very fine example of the Anglo-Saxon helmet referred to in chapter 2, was found by the late Mr. Bateman, in 1848, at Benty Grange, in Derbyshire. He says—

It was our good fortune to open a barrow which afforded a more instructive collection of relics than has ever been discovered in the country, and which are not surpassed in interest by any remains hitherto recovered from any Anglo-Saxon burial place in the kingdom.

Amongst these remains was the head-piece referred to. After describing the details of its structure, he adds—

On the crown of the helmet is an elliptical bronze plate supporting the figure of an animal carved in iron, with bronze eyes, now much corroded, but perfectly distinct as the representation of a hog.

www.ingramcontent.com/pod-product-compliance
Lightning Source LLC
Chambersburg PA
CBHW021105090426
42738CB00006B/508